OHIO

ONLINE

OHIO
ONLINE

The Harvest of Ohio's
Best Web Sites

By *Barbara Brattin*

ORANGE FRAZER *Press*
WILMINGTON, OHIO

ISBN: 1-882203-18-6
Copyright 1998 by Barbara Brattin
All rights reserved

Illustrations by Margaret Cresci
Cover art by Carol Benioff

Additional copies of *Ohio Online: The Harvest of Ohio's Best Web Sites* or other Orange Frazer Press publications may be ordered directly from:

Orange Frazer Press, Inc.
Box 214
37 ¹/₂ West Main Street
Wilmington, Ohio 45177

Telephone 1.800.852.9332 for price and shipping information
Web Site: www.orangefrazer.com; E-mail address: editor@orangefrazer.com

The information in this edition was compiled from the most current data available. Any errors, inaccuracies, or omissions are strictly unintentional.

Library of Congress Cataloging-in-Publication Data

Brattin, Barbara (Barbara Christine), 1958-
     Ohio online : the harvest of Ohio's best web sites/ by Barbara
Brattin
     p.   cm.
     ISBN 1-882203-18-6 (pbk.)
     1. Web sites—Ohio—Directories.   I. Title.
ZA4226.B73   1998
025.04—dc21   97-40012
                                                                    CIP

*For librarians everywhere
who work so hard to make
freedom of information
a reality.*

TABLE *of* CONTENTS

PREFACE

National online services are successful because they take the staggering amount of information available on the Internet and digest it into neat little categories of information for easier access. For the average Internet user, this is not only desirable, it is vital. Without these categories few users would know where to begin. In a matter of minutes, novice users can be updated on world and national events, sports scores, and hollywood entertainment. America is online, but where is the local information?

Local information is the most useful and desired information on the Internet. Americans want to know local high school football schedules, local job information, local news, and travel conditions. They want to locate this information from the comfort of home and do it any time, any day of the week. Yet there exists no printed "yellow pages" for internet sites specific to the regions and states where every American lives.

Ohio Online, the first of a multivolume, regional Internet directories series, will begin to fill that gap and bring Ohioans information they can use in their daily lives. Interested in researching your ancestry? *Ohio Online* guides you to local genealogical societies instantly. Planning your next vacation? *Ohio Online* has all the scoop on Ohio cities, camping and fishing sites, lodging and travel news. Looking for activities to occupy your children? *Ohio Online* takes your kids into the world of discovery with science and nature, games, puzzles, sports, educational challenges and more.

Sure, you could find any of this information using one of many web search engines. But with over 250,000 sites on the Internet to wade through and different search techniques for each search engine, the process becomes both difficult and imprecise. In short, search engines are not user-friendly.

Recently, I saw a short advertisement for a lecture at the Ohio Historical Center that held a particular appeal for me, but I was unsure of the center's hours and admission price for the lecture. It was 6pm on Friday and when I called the center it had already closed for the day, leaving a recorded message. I wound up calling several times long-distance because I had made the wrong menu choices, and after two calls, I still did not have the information I needed. I decided to use my Internet connection, and jumping right to a metasearcher for the best results, I got 954 matches to my query, "Ohio Historical Center". (Later, when, for curiosity's sake, I used Webcrawler, the default search engine for America Online, I got 171,555 hits.) Finally, I simply went to the OPLIN home page, whose URL (Universal Resource Locator) I knew, and which, I knew from experience, had a link to the OHS page. That's a long way to travel to get to the information you need, and for most Internet users, it would have been even longer.

Ohio Online puts URL's at your fingertips for instant, complete, and updated information 24 hours a day, 7 days a week. No wading through search engine hits, no long distance calls to dead end recordings. Just type in the URL on whatever online service you're using, and you're where you want to be — instantly.

Why start with Ohio? Surely there are more glitzy states with greater market appeal. The answer is the Ohio Public Library Information Network (OPLIN). Funded by the state of Ohio, OPLIN has successfully provided Internet access to all 249 public library systems and 700 library buildings in Ohio and every citizen within access of a library, whether in person or via modem. The Cleveland Public Library, the second largest public library in the United States, and its consortium of 28 public libraries in northern Ohio, provide dial-up access free of charge to more than a million residents each day. No other program like OPLIN exists in the U.S. today. OPLIN is the prototype for every state to wire its communities and provide access to all its citizens. Ohio is an Internet leader.

As a professional librarian, I work with hundreds of clients each week, providing Internet instruction and guidance to the best and worst on the net. Information about Ohio is of primary concern to my clients, yet the majority of them are unaware of how to find specific sites. They surf because they cannot drive. Confused by the concept of a search engine, or unwilling to master search techniques, I watch them link from site to site, seldom landing on the information they set out to find. So great is the need for direction that we have moved Internet directories adjacent to our search stations. They are devoured.

Savvy clients bring in clippings from magazines or newspapers with URL's they want to try. *Ohio Online*, an entire book of URL's, is the fastest, most efficient way to get to employment information, local weather, Ohio history, colleges and universities, the arts, the islands, parks, political action, environmental issues, real estate, Ohio cities, and the latest news across the state. It's all at one's fingertips. It's all in *Ohio Online*.

I. Introduction

Getting Online in Ohio

Here's the good news. If you live in Ohio you are already connected. The Ohio Public Library Information Network, with funding from the state of Ohio, has provided internet access to 249 public library systems representing more than 700 sites across the state. Bottom line: Free and equal Internet access to all Ohio citizens. In many libraries this means anyone coming off the street can walk up to a library terminal and begin searching. Other libraries, in response to the threat of vandalism or community concern over Internet content, require some sort of registration before a user may sign on. Check with your local library for their Internet policy. If you're just starting to learn about the Internet, this is a perfect way to preview it. Many libraries offer orientation classes.

Many people are interested in connecting to the internet from their home computers. There are a variety of ways to do this, and your choice will depend on what you want to do from home, such as sending or receiving electronic mail, joining listservs, communicating through chat rooms, or simply finding information. Another part of your choice will be whether you'll be satisfied with reading text files or desire to view the glitzy, graphic-laden sites on the World Wide Web. A third consideration will be cost. Following are three basic levels of home Internet access ranging from free to billed services:

Dial-up Access

Many Libraries offer a dial-up service whereby remote users may dial their modems to the library's server and receive access to the library online catalog. In the case of a library with a web catalog, dialing in puts the remote user on the Internet itself, allowing him to link to sites other than the library. If the dial-up number is a local call, this equates to free Internet access. Libraries rarely, however, provide e-mail service. Luckily there are several free e-mail providers on the Internet, including *hotmail* (http://www.hotmail.com) and *rocketmail* (http://www.rocketmail.com). Whether dial-up allows the user to see graphics or text-based files only, however, depends on the library's server, and may limit use of free e-mail services. Check with your local library for details.

FREE-NETS

Free-nets are exactly that — places to visit the Internet for free. By dialing in, users may access local information including business listings, school sites, government information, weather and job listings. Most free-nets offer e-mail to registered borrowers. There are at least 10 free net systems in Ohio:

AKRON COMMUNITY ONLINE RESOURCE NETWORK (ACORN)
Gopher://freenet.akron.oh.us/
dial up 330-643-9145

Akron InfoLine, a referral to community services, and the Family Friendly Akron Database, a link to all social service agencies in the Akron area, are two of the many useful links you'll find here. Ohio census data, Internet business links, and job opportunities can also be accessed.

CLEVELAND FREE-NET
http://cnswww.cns.cwru.edu/net/easy/fn/
dial-up 216-368-3888

This is the oldest free-net in the country, started in 1986. Medical information, local government, schools, libraries, and businesses are all linked to this large community network maintained by Case Western Reserve University.

DAYTON FREE-NET
http://130.108.128.174
dial-up 513-229-4373

GREATER COLUMBUS FREE-NET

http://www.freenet.columbus.oh.us/

dial-up 614-292-7501

Ohio State University hosts this project with help from the Ohio Supercomputer Center. Access the Columbus Job Connection, the Columbus Dispatch, education, health, and government sites around the state and nationwide. OSU electronic magazine is available, plus the university library catalog.

LAKE COUNTY FREE-NET

http://www.lakecountyfn.org/

Visit "Townsquare" for local educational sites, events, human services, politics, sports, and transportation information.

SOUTHEASTERN OHIO REGIONAL FREE-NET (SEORF)

http://www.seorf.ohiou.edu/

dial-up 614-593-1438, 1439, or 1136

Links to local schools, political groups, support groups, area health care, clubs, newspapers, and chamber of commerce. Includes a small business development center link.

TOLEDO FREE-NET

http://fnet.cc.utoledo.edu

TriState Online

http://www.tso.org/

dial-up 513-579-1990

This network serving Indiana, Ohio and Kentucky, features the Cincinnati Enquirer, the state-funded health database NetWellness, local television and radio stations, and universities.

WOOD COUNTY FREE-NET

http://www.wcnet.org/

contact 419-354-2727 for dial-up info

Daycare providers, preschools, private and public school systems, Wood County libraries, agricultural links, and health care facilities.

YOUNGSTOWN FREE-NET

http://gopher://yfn.ysu.edu/

Local business links, courthouses, churches, hospitals and doctors offices, library systems, newspapers, television, and radio stations. Find a pen pal, send e-mail, read the computer bulletin board, or the Youngstown State University animal hospital answers to common pet questions.

ISP's (INTERNET SERVICE PROVIDERS)

For those of you willing to fork over a little cash each month, this is the way to have it all: e-mail, chat rooms, listservs, world wide web, and even a place for your own home page. Rural residents may have few ISP's to choose from, since few may offer local dial-in numbers in the area. For a list of ISP's by area code, visit the directory at http://www.thedirectory.org/. Often word of mouth is the best way to shop for an ISP. Ask your friends and neighbors which service they use and whether they are satisfied.

Building Your Own Community Network

As of 1996 there were 500 community networks across the United States. At some point, community members decided such a network would be useful, whether as a way to promote a sense of community where none existed, to strengthen or revitalize one that did, or simply to provide a repository for local information. How did they begin such a daunting task? Where did they get the money, the technology, and who maintains the network that now exists?

In *New Community Networks: Wired for Change*, Douglas Schuler addresses the issues involved in setting up a community network. First, Schuler explains, decide your purpose. How will the network change the way your citizens communicate? Will these changes all be positive, or are there negative consequences you can foresee? Second, give your community a sense of ownership by involving everyone in the network's development. Successful community networks are people-based networks and you may dissipate unanticipated opposition by letting all parties provide input in the early stages of planning.

Next, decide on a starting point — the local library, local college, school, or government agency may already have a web presence and be willing to act as the launching pad for the community network. Although you may wish to offer free access to your users, building and maintaining the network will not be free — you will require some source of financial backing. How will you fund the project? Direct user fees, advertisers, donations, public funding, or a combination of the above? Each of the many networks in existence today uses one or more of these methods. Analyze your community resources and develop a clear plan of what advantages your network will offer to potential funding sources before you begin your finance campaign. What services will you offer? Most networks offer e-mail, some offer listservs, chat rooms and mailing list services. Will you provide dial-in service in addition to a local web site?

No one but your community can decide the answers to these issues you will face as you begin to build your community network. Each community has a unique character that will determine what type of network will serve its needs. Once you have made the necessary planning, budgeting, and management decisions, you'll need to select links to your new web site. *Ohio Online* is the perfect starting point. Read on.

II. One-Stop Web Sites

There are several Ohio-related sites that contain so many links to so many subject areas that they truly are one-stop sites for many needs. All you need is time and you can link to just about anything that has to do with Ohio.

City.Net Ohio

http://www.city.net/

City Net is a megasite that covers all of North America. The home page for Ohio lists links to area attractions, education, events, lodging, magazines, parks, weather, and maps. Relocation information, yellow pages, and links to major cities make this site particularly useful to those on the move, and families will enjoy the family events calendar links to regions of Ohio.

OhioBiz

http://www.ohiobiz.com

Available in English and 6 foreign languages, this site is graphically gorgeous and informationally outstanding. Geared toward Ohio business, this site also lists links to Ohio sports, transportation, media, education, travel, cities, Ohio jobs, and government. "Postcards from Ohio" contains daily updates, and featured sites change periodically. Ohio businesses are highlighted and a section called Resource Ohio lists programs, incentives, and assistance available to Ohio businesses.

OHIO PUBLIC LIBRARY INFORMATION NETWORK (OPLIN)

http://www.oplin.lib.oh.us

The brainchild of Ohio library leaders, and funded by the Ohio state government, OPLIN was created to "ensure equity of access to information for all Ohio citizens." What it has achieved is astounding. Every Ohio public library and the populations they serve enjoy Internet access thanks to the vision of OPLIN. What you will find when you enter this site will amaze you—everything you need to know about Ohio's history, government, schools, and libraries, links to travel and cultural sites across the state, plus listings of business and entertainment sites in Ohio. The current events page will keep you abreast of state and national events in the making, and the OHKids! page links the best of the web for children. In addition to what's available from your home computer, citizens using the OPLIN website in an Ohio public library can access databases including newspaper and magazine indexes, HANNAH, the state's index to Ohio legislation, and Novelist, a database that matches fiction titles to readers' tastes.

III. Cities

The home pages of Ohio cities hold an enormous amount of information specific to their communities. Here is where you will find shopping, local businesses, restaurants, links to area schools, city services, regulations and ordinances. If you're traveling through a small city not found in the larger Ohio travel sites, come to their home page for a great introduction to the people, the landscape, and the culture.

GENERAL CITY SITES

NORTHEAST OHIO SITES ONLINE
http://neohio.sitesonline.com/
Although Cleveland has its own version of this site, the northeast site focuses heavily on its largest city as well. This site is a collection of business, health, media, sports, retail, and entertainment links for the northeast area of the state. Cities with web pages are listed in the community section.

CITY NET OHIO
http://www.city.net/
This index starts out globally, so you need to work your way down to Ohio listings. Each city choice lists its home page and/or any other web page from the area.

Northwest Ohio Sites Online

http://nwohio.sitesonline.com/

All the links from government to education, entertainment and shopping for the northwest region of the state. Includes links to cities with web pages in the region.

Ohiolink Community Place

http://www.ohio-link.com/

Choose community place and you'll get a list of city links to choose from.

Virtual Ohio

http://www.virtual-ohio.com/

Home pages for many cities in Ohio are gathered together on this page. Frames make them not quite as easy to view as the original pages, but if you're just browsing, this is a good place to start.

City Home Pages

Akron-The All-American City

http://config.akron.oh.us/

Links to the most popular sites around Akron.

Athens

http://www.seorf.ohiou.edu/~xx061/

A true community site, with information on recycling, after school care, rental properties, city department functions, even a phone directory.

BEAVERCREEK

http://www.hcst.net/beavercreek/

Demographics, history, local shopping, schools, and community organizations.

BEDFORD

http://www.virtcity.com/cities/bedford/

Community life, city government departments and services, and churches are all featured here.

BELLEVUE

http://www.nwoh.com/sites/bellevue.htm

Business, school, and shopping links, plus information on area attractions and recreational opportunites.

BERLIN HEIGHTS

http://www.berlinheights.com/

Education, business, clubs, and government links.

BRECKSVILLE

http://www.virtcity.com/cities/brecksvi/

Area attractions, city departments, businesses, schools and restaurants, plus a city map.

BROADVIEW HEIGHTS

http://www.virtcity.com/cities/broadvie/home.html

City department links, fun sites, recreation, real estate, restaurants, plus a map of the area.

BROOK PARK

http://www.virtcity.com/cities/brookpark/

Internet white pages, a virtual map, school and recreational links, plus government services.

BRUNSWICK

http://www.brunswick.oh.us/

This small town has an accomplished web page, with links to elected officials, health care facilities, newspapers, tax information, and census statistics. Includes the Brunswick Zoning Code.

BRYAN

http://www.bryanworld.com/

This is a lovely community web site, with links to anything and everything in the Bryan area and a chat room for area residents.

BUCYRUS

http://www.mindspring.com/~lazydog/bucyrus/bucyrus.htm

The Bratwurst Capital of America brings you business, health, and government links.

CANFIELD

http://www.cisnet.com/~canfield/

History of the city, links to officials, a special events calendar, and an online church directory are just a few of the things you'll find on this web site.

CANTON

http://www.canton-ohio.com/

Everything you need to know about Canton and surrounding communities, including links to the Canton Pro Football Hall of Fame and Festival, service clubs, education, religion, media and entertainment.

CELINA

http://www.bright.net/~cmu/

This web site is so pretty it makes you want to move there. Lots of links to keep you informed about the city and area.

CENTERVILLE

http://www.dnaco.net/~bkottman/Centerville/

Area businesses, schools, parks, plus the Centerville High School Alumni Page.

CHILLICOTHE

http://brightnet.horizontel.com/chilli/

This is quite an extensive site with links to a lot of great information for the area. For the politically active, this site features links to contact government officials, radio stations, TV stations, and newspapers with your comments. A map of Chillicothe is included.

CINCINNATI INTERNET COMMUNITY

http://www.cincinnati.com

This is a huge entertainment site with links to restaurants, arts and nightlife.

CINCINNATI USA

http://cincyusa.com/

The home page of the Cincinnati Convention and Visitors Bureau, this site links to conventions, sports events, attractions, dining, and accommodations in Cincinnati.

CINCY.COM

http://www.cincy.com

This page has links to everything you can think of in and around Cincinnati, including real estate, schools, libraries, businesses, arts, news, even geography.

CLEVELAND — ACCESS CLEVELAND

http://www.clevelandohio.com/

Information on what to do and where to go, including categories like shops, services, nightlife, leisure, wanted, and for sale.

CLEVELAND LIVE

http://www.cleveland.com/

A great entertainment site for Cleveland and vicinity with links to area cities, contests, surveys, sports reports, and feature articles.

CLEVELAND NEIGHBORHOOD LINK

http://www.nhlink.net/

This site takes the distinctly different Cleveland neighborhood areas and lists community resources, news and events within each.

CLEVELAND NET

http://www.apk.net/cleveland/

Area events, lifestyles, entertainment, sweepstakes, and business information.

Cleveland Sites Online

http://cleveland.sitesonline.com/

There are so many sites for Cleveland. This one has links to everything from business to culture and adds seasonal features to boot.

Cleveland — The New American City

http://www.cleveland.oh.us/

The Official Greater Cleveland Homepage, this is entertainment link heaven with links to restaurants, nightlife, and sports teams. Includes maps.

Coldwater

http://www.bright.net/~coldwatr/

Lists of village officials and departments, area business and industry, plus individuals and families. Includes a location map.

Columbus Metroscope

http://metroscope.com/columbus.html

This large collection of Columbus links includes colleges, arts, business, media, and government, plus a Columbus guide and list of Internet and professional services.

Columbus Pages

http://www.columbuspages.com/

It's just like reading the newspaper, with links to comics, calendar, sports, news, weather, and business news. If you're looking for entertainment, this site includes a movie guide.

COLUMBUS SUPERSITE
http://www.columbus.org

This is truly a supersite, listing employment, arts, education, government, media, organizations and more.

DAYTON HOME PAGE
http://www.dayton.net/dayton

Community events, weather, schools, politics, history, and business in the Dayton area.

DEFIANCE
http://www.defianceweb.com/

Realty, restaurants, area churches and education all find a home on this page, as well as community events and the Fort Defiance chat room. Includes a directory to e-mail and web pages in the Defiance area.

DELAWARE
http://www.delaware.org/

Classified ads, visitors bureau, and community links.

DELPHOS
http://www.delphos-ohio.com

Area maps, business links, events calendar, and town history.

DRESDEN
http://www.dresdenohio.com

The "Basket Capital of the World" offers a chat room, city history, and business directory on its home page.

DUBLIN
http://www.dublin.oh.us/

This unique site offers a choice among city services, recreation, events and an online resident guide featuring city ordinances and voting information.

EAST LIVERPOOL
http://www.eastliverpool.com/

The "Pottery Capital of the World" gives us a regional map, calendar of community events, plus a guide to recreation, dining, and accommodations.

EASTLAKE
http://ci.eastlake.oh.us

Take a virtual tour, read council minutes, get city tax information, check business and restaurant guides.

EDGERTON
http://www.bright.net/~dekrill/Edgerton.html

History, location, demographics, plus Ohio links.

ELMORE
http://www.elmore.oh.us/

This village home page has links to the entire community — business, schools, library, and local attractions, plus a local history photo gallery and village map.

FAIRBORN
http://ci.fairborn.oh.us/city/cityindex.html

Parks and recreation, frequently asked questions, city departments, and information about how to reach city officials.

FLATSNET

http://www.flats.net

Online guide to the entertainment, restaurants, bars and nightlife in the restored flats area of Cleveland's downtown. Includes a parking map to give you the edge on limited spaces.

FOSTORIA

http://www.fostoria.gov/

Links to elected and administrative officials, including council meeting schedule, plus a short history of Fostoria.

FREMONT

http://www.fremontohio.org

This site provides an online visitors guide, fire insurance rating for the city, plus links to civic groups, churches, area sports, schools, and Fremont history.

GAHANNA

http://www.gahanna.k12.oh.us/city

Choose links from a city map leading to the mayor's office, zoning, chamber of commerce, police, or schools.

GALION

http://sketch.com/galion/

History and demographics, plus a city map.

GALLIPOLIS

http://www.gallipolis.org

The city's history is explained, and city departments are linked describing their services. Tax rates for the area are included.

GARFIELD HEIGHTS

http://garfieldhts.com/

Each city department has its own home page describing its function. This site includes a map of the city and an e-mail link to send messages to your elected officials.

GENEVA-ON-THE-LAKE

http://www.ncweb.com/gol/

This is a resort town and you can tell by its web page. Attractions, maps, and an accommodations directory are included.

GIRARD

http://www.girard.lib.oh.us/city.htm

Each city department is listed with its own link describing services to area residents. An online phone directory is included.

GRANVILLE

http://www.granville.oh.us/

Join the community discussion, read proposed legislation or council meeting minutes.

GREENFIELD

http://www.greenfield-ohio.com

Real estate, medical facilities, local news and weather, plus Greenfield emergency resources.

GROVE CITY

http://www.ci.grove-city.oh.us/

Links to the public library, city government, and chamber of commerce.

Hamilton

http://www.hamilton-ohio.com/

Area arts, history, sports, shopping, festivals, maps and mileage.

Hicksville

http://www.cclass.com/hicks/

You could be the next person of the week on this web site. Businesses, schools, medical providers, news, restaurants, shopping and the local county fair are all highlighted.

Holland

http://www.primenet.com/~vholland

This site includes northwest Ohio links, a location map, business index, and an e-mail link to village officials.

Independence

http://organizations.44131.com/city

A nice description of the city, plus a calendar of events and list of organizations.

Indian Lake

http://indianlake.com

A very pleasant page advertising the recreational opportunities in the Indian Lake area. Includes maps, business and shopping links.

Lakewood

http://www.lkwdpl.org/city

History, links to city council and courts, and city offices.

LANCASTER

http://members.aol.com/LancOH/

Join the chat room, search the business directory, link to search engines, schools, and government departments.

LEBANON

http://ourworld.compuserve.com/homepages/leboh

Links to area attractions and city departments.

LIMA

http://www.cityhall.lima.oh.us/

Citizens may pay their water bills online and check city job opportunities.

MANSFIELD/RICHLAND COUNTY

http://www.richnet.net/richland/

Jobs, real estate, weather, local government, and businesses, plus a link to local newsgroups.

MARION

http://www.marion.net/

This site has it all — yellow pages, history, genealogy, tourism, business, and education.

MASSILLON

http://www.rickohio.com/massillon/city.htm

Tigertown is represented here with links to the Massillon Tiger Football Home Page, historic sites, and area newspaper sports pages.

MAYFIELD HEIGHTS

http://www.intheworld.com/mh/

This site has some unique features. Download forms such as garage sale applications, list real estate property free of charge, or read city meeting minutes.

MAYFIELD VILLAGE

http://www.mayfieldvillage.com

Rules and regulations for this village are online, plus information on each village government unit.

MEDINA

http://www.medina.net

Read the city's history, census information and school information.

MIDDLETOWN

http://www.middletown.com

In addition to area business and tourism information, this site includes links to local organizations, schools, churches, and employment opportunities.

MINERVA

http://www.minervaohio.com/

Guide to local businesses and resources.

NEWTON FALLS

http://www.newtonfalls.lib.oh.us/com/index.htm

This is a very well organized home page, with categories ranging from education to voting and elections. This page is part of the Newton Falls Community Network which includes links to the local library and other interesting web sites.

North Olmsted

http://www.ci.north-olmsted.oh.us/

Download building permits or tax exemption forms, check city events, services, and link to local schools.

Norwalk

http://www.accnorwalk.com/credits/norwalk/chamber1.html

The "Maple City's" home page includes local government, schools and tourism information, plus an online business directory.

Orrville

http://www.orrville.com

Orrville's city charter is online, along with a list of elected officials, and a history of the city.

Oxford

http://www.oxford-online.com/

You can tell this is a college town. Rentals, bars, and classifieds are featured links along with restaurants and vacation information.

Parma

http://www.virtcity.com/cities/parma/

History, government services, schools, recreation, and local hospital information, plus a map of the city.

Parma Heights

http://www.virtcity.com/cities/parmahts/

Real estate, parks, businesses, senior services, schools, plus links to city hall.

PERRYSBURG

http://www.perrysburg.com/

Current news and weather, plus links to local schools, business and government.

PIQUA

http://www.wesnet.com/piquaoh/

Citizens may e-mail their elected officials from this page, or link to any of the city services.

PORT CLINTON

http://www.lake-erie.com/portc.htm

Ah, the lake. This site describes the beauty of this northern area.

PUT-IN-BAY

http://www.primenet.com/~jblatt/pib2.html

Events, fishing information, saloons, and transportation to the island.

SALEM

http://www.salemohio.com/

History of the city, links to the public library, local government, and community news and events.

SANDUSKY

http://www.peoplevision.com/

All the local links you'd expect, plus Cedar Point, Microsoft, ESPN, Yahoo, and chat rooms.

SHAKER HEIGHTS

http://www.shaker-hts.oh.us/

How did Shaker Heights get its name? What is community life like there? What are the schools like, the homes? This page will answer all these questions plus link you to city hall.

SPRINGFIELD

http://www.ci.springfield.oh.us/

Links to each city department, plus Springfield heritage, economic and trade information.

ST. MARYS

http://rocky.bright.net/stmarys/

Industrial and commercial sites, tourism, plus a community profile.

STEUBENVILLE

http://www.microprosys.com/steubenville/

Real estate guide, public forum, and business and community center links for the "City of Murals."

STOW

http://www.stow.oh.us/

General city information and city services.

SWANTON

http://village.swanton.oh.us/

Links to the public library, entertainment, business, clubs, and police, plus a community calendar.

SYLVANIA

http://www.sev.org/

A wonderful site. Come to the Sylvania Electronic Village and choose links to schools, library, news, recreation, city government, or other Internet sites.

TIFFIN

http://www.bpsom.com/tiffin.html

Demographics, schools, health care, government, industry, recreation — everything a citizen would need to know.

TOLEDO

http://www.toledo.com/

This is a large site for a large city, complete with cultural, business, government and education links.

TROTWOOD

http://www.trotwood.org/

This site was developed for citizen participation. Read the city goals and business newsletter, download a city map, or check a phone number.

TROY

http://www.erinet.com/troy/

Schools, festivals, health care and business links, plus a history of Miami County.

TWINSBURG

http://www.twinsburg.com/

Real estate, recreation, shopping, restaurants, and an online business directory. Includes information about the annual Twins Days held in this city.

University Heights

http://www.virtcity.com/cities/universityhts/

Businesses, city departments, schools and recreation in the "City of Beautiful Homes."

Van Wert

http://www.vanwert.com/

Organizations, events, and business links.

Venedocia

http://www.geocities.com/Heartland/Hills/2761

Street maps, photographs, local history and community events.

Vermilion

http://www.vermilionohio.com/

Community sports, local attractions, schools, area history, businesses and government are highlighted on this small town's home page.

Waterville

http://www.waterville.org/

This is a very pretty home page with many links to community including schools, area history, public services, and entertainment.

Westerville

http://www.geocities.com/~westerville/

This represents a well-developed community network with yellow pages, a kids page, student resource guide, and other Internet links.

WESTLAKE

http://www.virtcity.com/cities/westlake/

City services, parks, schools, community profile, city history, plus virtual white pages.

WICKLIFFE

http://www.virtcity.com/cities/wickliffe/

In addition to an online business directory and area map, this site links to area schools, recreation, recycling information, and city council meeting schedule.

WILLOUGHBY

http://www.virtcity.com/cities/willoughby/

Internet white pages, city departments, schools, recreation and an area map.

WILLOWICK

http://www.virtcity.com/cities/willowick/

What's new in Willowick? This page covers it all — business, city government, schools and recreation.

WILMINGTON

http://www.postcom.com/wilmington/

Find out why Wilmington has been rated one of the best small towns in America by visiting this lovely web site, complete with a directory of local officials, location map, city profile, and a host of related sites.

WOOD COUNTY CITIES

http://www.wcnet.org/gov/

Most of these cities are too small to have their own home page, but the community network has given them each a spot to describe their cities and services.

WOODVILLE

http://www.toledolink.com/~dlare/woodville/

History of the city, plus links to schools and business.

WORTHINGTON

http://www.worthington.org

Links to schools, library, community and business, plus a calendar of events.

YELLOW SPRINGS

http://www.visityellowsprings.com

Area events and attractions, plus directions for visitors.

YOUNGSTOWN/ MAHONING VALLEY

http://members.aol.com/fixtron/page.htm

Attractions, sports, arts, and industry, including some nearby Pennsylvania sites.

ZANESVILLE

http://www.zanesville-ohio.com

This "supersite" features area maps, links of interest, a community profile, calendar of events, and business directory.

IV. Media

Every newspaper, television and radio station in Ohio has found a home on the Internet. What started as merely a form of publicity has blossomed into full coverage of today's news stories online, classifieds for all areas of the state, and live radio programs broadcast over the net. It doesn't matter where you live anymore, or how far the frequency will carry, the whole state is at your fingertips.

NEWSPAPERS

For the big picture, turn to Ohio Newslink (page 41), a compilation of news stories from all over the state.

DAILIES & WEEKLIES

AKRON BEACON JOURNAL
http://www.beaconjournal.com/

ASHTABULA STAR BEACON
http://www.ashtabula.net/StarBeacon/

Athens Messenger

http://www.athens-messenger.com/

Athens News

http://www.athensnews.com/

Aurora Advocate

http://www.recordpub.com/aa/

Bedford Times-Register

http://www.recordpub.com/btr

Canton Repository

http://www.cantonrespository.com/

Chagrin Valley Times

http://www.chagrinvalleytimes.com/

Cincinnati CityBeat

http://www.citybeat.com/

Cincinnati Enquirer

http://www.enquirer.com

Cincinnati Everybody's News

http://www.everybodys.org/

Cincinnati Herald

http://www.cincyherald.com/

Cincinnati Post

http://www.cincypost.com

CLEVELAND FREE TIMES

http://www.freetimes.com

CLEVELAND LIVE

http://www.cleveland.com/

CLEVELAND SUN NEWSPAPERS

http://www.sunnews.com

CLINTON COUNTY POST

http://www.postcom.com/ccpost/

COLUMBUS ALIVE

http://www.alivewired.com

COLUMBUS DISPATCH

http://www.dispatch.com

COLUMBUS FREE PRESS

http://www.freepress.org/home.html

CUYAHOGA FALLS NEWS-PRESS

http://www.recordpub.com/cfnp/

DELAWARE GAZETTE

http://www.delgazette.com/

EAST LIVERPOOL REVIEW ONLINE

http://www.reviewonline.com/

EATON REGISTER-HERALD

http://www.registerherald.com

ELYRIA CHRONICLE TELEGRAM

http://www.ohio.net/~ect/

FINDLAY COURIER

http://www.thecourier.com/

GATEWAY NEWS (STREETSBORO AREA)

http://www.recordpub.com/tgn/

HAMILTON JOURNAL-NEWS

http://www.journal-news.com/home.cfm

HOLMES COUNTY HUB

http://www.amish-heartland.com/thehub/

KENT/ RAVENNA RECORD-COURIER

http://www.recordpub.com/rc

LAKE LEADER

http://www.recordpub.com/ll/

LANCASTER EAGLE-GAZETTE

http://www.eagle-gazette.com/

LIMA NEWS

http://www.limanews.com

LORAIN MORNING JOURNAL

http://www.centuryinter.net/oh/journal/index.html

MAPLE HEIGHTS PRESS

http://www.recordpub.com/mh/

Martins Ferry Times-Leader

http://www.oweb.com/times_leader/

Medina County Gazette

http://www.medina-gazette.com/

Middletown JournaLink

http://journalink.com/

News Leader (Macedonia Area)

http://www.recordpub.com/nl/

Open Market (Tiffin)

http://om.bpsom.com/

Oxford Press

http://www.oxfordpress.com/

Perrysburg Messenger Journal

http://www.perrysburg.com/welch/index.htm

Press (Avon Lake)

http://www.bright.net/~thepress/

Sandusky Register

http://www.sanduskyregister.com/html/home.htm

Steubenville Herald-Star

http://www.hsconnect.com/home.html

Stow Sentry

http://www.recordpub.com/ss/

Sun Newspapers

http://www.sunnews.com

Sunbury News

http://www.sunburynews.com/

Tallmadge Express

http://www.recordpub.com/te

Tiffin Advertiser Tribune

http://www.oweb.com/advertiser-tribune

Twinsburg Bulletin

http://www.recordpub.com/tb/

Wapakoneta Daily News

http://www.bright.net/~wapakwdn/wdn.html

Warren Tribune-Chronicle

http://www.tribune-chronicle.com/

Yellow Springs News

http://www.ysnews.com

Business

Akron Legal News

http://www.akronlegalnews.com/

CINCINNATI BUSINESS COURIER
http://www.amcity.com/cincinnati/index.html

CLEVELAND CRAIN'S BUSINESS
http://www.crainscleveland.com

COLUMBUS BUSINESS FIRST
http://www.amcity.com/columbus/index.html

COLUMBUS DAILY REPORTER
http://www.sddt.com/~columbus/index.html

DAYTON BUSINESS REPORTER
http://www.daytonbusiness.com/index.asp

YOUNGSTOWN BUSINESS JOURNAL
http://www.business-journal.com

COLLEGE/UNIVERSITY PAPERS

BLUFFTON COLLEGE WITMARSUM
http://www.bluffton.edu/witmarsum/

CINCINNATI NEWS RECORD
http://www.uc.edu/www/newsrecord/index.htmlx

KENYON COLLEGIAN
http://topaz.kenyon.edu/pubs/collegian/

MARIETTA COLLEGE MARCOLIAN

http://www.marietta.edu/~marc/index.html

MOUNT UNION COLLEGE DYNAMO

http://207.1.36.53/

MUSKINGUM COLLEGE BLACK AND MAGENTA

http://www.muskingum.edu/~black/

OBERLIN REVIEW

http://www.oberlin.edu/~ocreview/

OHIO STATE UNIVERSITY LANTERN

http://www.thelantern.com

OHIO UNIVERSITY POST

http://132.235.238.184/

OHIO WESLEYAN UNIVERSITY TRANSCRIPT

http://www.owu.edu/~owunews/index.html

UNIVERSITY OF AKRON BUCHTELITE

http://www.uakron.edu/buchtelite

UNIVERSITY OF DAYTON FLYER NEWS

http://www.udayton.edu/~flynews/

UNIVERSITY OF TOLEDO COLLEGIAN

http://www.utoledo.edu/www/collegian/

XAVIER UNIVERSITY NEWSWIRE

http://www.xu.edu/soa/newswire/

OTHER

OHIO NEWSLINK

http://www.oweb.com/newslink/ohio/
Links to news stories from all over the state.

OHIO NEWSPAPER INDEXES

http://winslo.ohio.gov/ohnewsindex.html

TELEVISION STATIONS

Public Broadcasting stations are marked with an asterik.

*WOUB/WOUC ATHENS

http://www.tcom.ohiou.edu/tv.html

*WBGU BOWLING GREEN

http://www-wbgu.bgsu.edu/

WWHO-TV CHILLICOTHE

http://www.wb53.com/

*WCET CINCINNATI

http://www.iglou.com/wcet/

WCPO-TV CINCINNATI

http://www.wcpo.com/

WBNX-TV CLEVELAND

http://www.wbnx.com

WJW-TV CLEVELAND

http://www.zdepth.com/wjw/

WBNS-TV COLUMBUS

http://www.wbns10tv.com/

WTTE-TV COLUMBUS

http://www.wtte.com

WCMH-TV COLUMBUS

http://www.wcmh4.com/

WDTN-TV DAYTON

http://www.wdtn.com/wdtn/

*WEAO/WNEO KENT

http://www.ch4549.org/

WTLW-TV LIMA

http://www.wtlw.com/

WTOV-TV STEUBENVILLE

http://www.ovnet.com/wtov9/

*WGTE TOLEDO

http://www.wgte.org/

WNWO-TV TOLEDO

http://www.nbc24.com/

WUPW-TV TOLEDO

http://www.wupw.com/

WTOL-TV TOLEDO

http://www.wtol.com/

WFMJ-TV YOUNGSTOWN

http://www.wfmj.com/

WKBN-TV YOUNGSTOWN

http://www.wkbn.com/news.htm

RADIO STATIONS

If your computer is running RealAudio, stand back. Many stations have background music.

ALTERNATIVE ROCK

WXTQ 105.5 FM ATHENS

http://www.eurekanet.com/~wxtq

WRQK 106.9 FM CANTON

http://www.wrqk.com

WAVE 94.9 FM CLEVELAND

http://www.949thewave.com/

WENZ 107.9 FM CLEVELAND

http://www.1079.com

WZJM 92.5 FM CLEVELAND

http://www.jammin.com/

WBZX 99.7 FM COLUMBUS

http://www.wbzx.com/theblitz/

WUFM 88.7 FM COLUMBUS

http://www.radiou.com/

WWCD 101.1 FM COLUMBUS

http://www.cd101.com/

WBUZ 106.5 FM DELTA

http://www.primenet.com/buzz/

WKXA 100.5 SM FINDLAY

http://www.findlayoh.com/wkxa/

WAQZ 107.1 FM MILFORD

http://www.channel-z.com/

WOXY 97.7 FM OXFORD

http://www.woxy97x.com/

WXKR 94.5 FM PORT CLINTON

http://www.primenet.com/~x945/

WSTB 88.9 STREETSBORO

http://www.889vrock.com

CLASSIC ROCK AND ROLL

WONE 97.5 FM AKRON
http://www.wone.net

WEBN 102.7 FM CINCINNATI
http://www.webn.com/

WMMS 100.7 FM CLEVELAND
http://www.wmms.com/wmms/

WNCX 98.5 FM CLEVELAND
http://www.wncx.com

WING 102.9 FM DAYTON
http://www.erinet.com/wingfm/start.html

WKET 98.3 FM DAYTON
http://wket.fm.net/

WTUE 104.7 FM DAYTON
http://www.arsdayton.com/wtue.html

WWJM 106.3 FM NEW LEXINGTON
http://www.wwjm.com

WQTL 106.3 FM OTTAWA
http://www.bright.net/~wqtl/

WCPZ 102.7 FM Sandusky

http://www.peoplevision.com/wcpzwlec/wcpz

WIOT 104.7 FM Toledo

http://www.wiot.com/

WNCD 106.1 FM Youngstown

http://www.cd106.com/

Top 40/ Light Rock

WKDD 96.5 FM Akron

http://www.wkdd.com

WFUN 970 AM Ashtabula

http://www.ashtabula.net/star97/

WREO 97.1 FM Ashtabula

http://www.ashtabula.net/star97/

WLTF 106.5 FM Cleveland

http://websites.radio-online.com/wltf/index.htm

WQAL 104.1 FM Cleveland

http://www.q104.com/

WGTZ 92.3 FM Dayton

http://www.wgtz.com

WDFM 98.1 FM DEFIANCE

http://www.bright.net/~wdfm/

WJER 101.7 FM DOVER

http://www.tusco.net/wjer/wjer/wjermain.htm

WBVI 96.7 FM FINDLAY

http://www.wbvi.com/mix967_home.html

WMMA 97.3 FM LEBANON

http://www.wmma.com/

WYHT 105.3 FM MANSFIELD

http://www.wyht.com/

WZIO 94.9 FM SOUTH WEBSTER

http://www.zoomnet.net/~wzio/

WWWM 105.5 FM SYLVANIA

http://www.105-fm.com/

WVKS 92.5 FM TOLEDO

http://www.toledolink.com/kissfm

WKSD 99.7 FM VAN WERT

http://www.vanwert.com/wert/

WHOT 101.1 FM YOUNGSTOWN

http://www.neont.com/whot101/whot.htm

WKBN 99.1 FM YOUNGSTOWN

http://www.wkbn.com/

WYFM 102.9 FM YOUNGSTOWN

http://www.y-103.com/

OLDIES

WFUN 970 AM ASHTABULA

http://www.ashtabula.net/wfun/

WZKL 92 FM CANTON

http://www.canton-ohio.com/wzkl/wzkl.html

WGRR 103.5 FM CINCINNATI

http://www.wgrr1035.com/

WBNS 97.1 FM COLUMBUS

http://www.oldiesb97.com/

WCLR 95.7 FM DAYTON

http://www.kool95.com/

WONE 980 AM DAYTON

http://www.arsdayton.com/star98.html

WZLR 95.3 FM DAYTON

http://www.kool95.com/

WBUK 107.5 FM LIMA

http://www.wbuk.com

WNKO 101.7 FM NEWARK

http://www.wnko.com/

WIOI 1010 AM PORTSMOUTH

http://www.zoomnet.net/~wioi/index.html

WERT 1220 AM VAN WERT

http://vanwert.com/wert/

WBBG 93.3 FM YOUNGSTOWN

http://www.neont.com/oldies/oldies93.htm

WYBZ 107.3 FM ZANESVILLE

http://www.wybz.com/

TALK SHOWS

WBLL 1390 AM BELLEFONTAINE

http://www.wbll.com/

WFII 1230 AM COLUMBUS

http://1230fyi.com/

WTVN 610 AM COLUMBUS

http://www.wtvn.com/

WHIO 1290 AM DAYTON

http://www.aquinas-mutimedia.com/whio/

WELW 1330 AM Eastlake

http://datalink.bblink.com/welw/

WFOB 1430 AM Fostoria

http://www.wfob.com/

WCLT 1430 AM Newark

http://www.wclt.com/

WBKC 1460 AM Painesville

http://www.wbkc.com/

WSTV 1340 AM Steubenville

http://www.weir.net/wstv/

WRRO 1440 AM Warren

http://www.am1440.com/

WCHO 105.5 FM Washington Court House

http://www.washingtonch..com/wcho.htm

WKBN 570 AM Youngstown

http://www.wkbn.com/

Classical

WCLV 95.5 FM Cleveland

http://www.wclv.com/

NPR

WOUB 1340 AM, 91.3 FM Athens
http://www.tcom.ohiou.edu/pubradio/am-skd.html

WOUC 89.1 FM Cambridge
http://www.tcom.ohiou.edu/radio.html

WOUH 91.9 FM Chillicothe
http://www.tcom.ohiou.edu/radio.html

WVXC 89.3 FM Chillicothe
http://www.xstarnet.com/

WGUC 90.9 FM Cincinnati
http://www.pol.com/WGUC/

WVXU 91.7 FM Cincinnati
http://www.starnet.com/

WCBE 90.5 FM Columbus
http://wcbe.iwaynet.net

WKSU 89.7 FM Kent
http://www.wksu.kent.edu/

WVXG 95.1 FM Mt. Gilead
http://www.xstarnet.com/

WMUB 88.5 FM Oxford

http://www.muohio.edu/wmub/

WVXW 89.5 FM West Union

http://www.xstarnet.com

WYSO 91.3 FM Yellow Springs

http://www.wyso.org/

Country

WQMX 94.9 FM Akron

http://www.wqmx.com/

WBEX 1490 AM Chillicothe

http://www.wbex.com/

WKKJ 93.3 FM Chillicothe

http://www.wkkj.com/

WGAR 99.5 FM Cleveland

http://www.wgar.com/

WCOL 92.3 FM Columbus

http://wcol.com/

WHKO 99.1 FM Dayton

http://k99.1fm.erinet.com/

WWBK 98.3 FM FREDERICKTOWN

http://www.kcountry.com/

WKKY 104.7 FM GENEVA

http://www.wkky.com/

WBZW 107.7 FM LOUDONVILLE

http://www.kcountry.com/

WCLT 100.3 FM NEWARK

http://www.wclt.com/

WHTH 790 AM NEWARK

http://www.wnko.com/

WKSW 101.7 FM SPRINGFIELD

http://www.kisscountry.com/

WRKY 103.5 FM STEUBENVILLE

http://www.wrky.com/

WXIZ 100.9 FM WAVERLY

http://www.zoomnet.net/~wxiz/

JAZZ

WKHR 91.5 FM CHAGRIN FALLS

http://207.122.180.3/wkhr/

WVAE 94.9 FM Cincinnati

http://www.949thewave.com

WNWV 107.3 FM Elyria

http://www.wnwv.com/

College/University Stations

WRDL 88.9 FM Ashland University

http://www.ashland.edu/~wrdl/

WBGU 88.1 FM Bowling Green State University

http://ernie.bgsu.edu/~ckile/WBGUFMhome.html

WFAL 680 AM Bowling Green State University

http://www.bgsu.edu/studentlife/organizations/wfal/

WRUW 91.1 FM Case Western Reserve University

http://www.cwru.edu/orgs/wruw/wruw.html

WCDR 90.3 FM Cedarville College

http://www.cedarville.edu/dept/cdr/

WSRN 99.5 FM Cedarville College

http://www.cedarville.edu/student_org/u995fm/

WCSB 89.3 FM Cleveland State University

http://wcsb.org/

WMSR 540 AM MIAMI UNIVERSITY

http://www.muohio.edu/~wmsr/

WRMU 91.1 FM MOUNT UNION COLLEGE

http://www.muc.edu/cwis/groups/WRMU/WRMU.html

WOBC 91.5 FM OBERLIN

http://www.oberlin.edu/~WOBC/

WONB 94.9 FM OHIO NORTHERN UNIVERSITY

http://www.onu.edu/wonb/

KBUX 91.1 FM OHIO STATE UNIVERSITY

http://www.osu.edu/students/kbux/

WLHD 100.7 FM OHIO UNIVERSITY

http://oak.cats.ohiou.edu/~wlhd/

WDCR 1550 AM 98.1 FM UNIVERSITY OF DAYTON

http://www.udayton.edu/~flyer-radio/index.html

WXUT 88.3 FM UNIVERSITY OF TOLEDO

http://www.rec-center.utoledo.edu/wxut/index.html

WWSU 106.9 FM WRIGHT STATE UNIVERSITY

http://www.media.wright.edu/studorgs/wwsu/wwsuhome.htm

SPORTS

WAKR 1590 AM AKRON
http://www.wakr.net/

WKKI 94.3 FM CELINA
http://www.bright.net/~wkki/

WBOB 1160 AM CINCINNATI
http://www.1160bob.com/

WBNS 1460 AM COLUMBUS
http://www.radiohio.com/1460home.html

WLEC 1450 AM SANDUSKY
http://www.peoplevision.com/wcpzwlec/wlec

RAP/SOUL

WZAK 93.1 FM CLEVELAND
http://www.wzak.com/

WBTT 94.5 FM DAYTON
http://www.thebeat945.com

CHRISTIAN

WCRF 103.3 FM Cleveland
http://www.moody.edu/MBN/WCRF/

WFCJ 93.7 FM Dayton
http://www.wfcj.com/

WQRP 88.1 FM Dayton
http://www.wqrp.org/

WGNZ 1110 AM Fairborn
http://www.good-news.org/

WNLT 104.3 FM Harrison
http://www.wnlt.com/

WTRJ 96.9 FM Troy
http://www.donet.com/wtrj/wtrj.htm

WXIC 660 AM Waverly
http://www.zoomnet.net/~wxic/

V. Sports

Ohio has a large number of professional and semi-pro teams covering a wide variety of sports from soccer to hockey, football, baseball, and stock car racing. This year, Ohio takes the lead with the introduction of a professional women's basketball team in Cleveland and semi-pro women's baseball teams in Akron and Columbus. Cincinnati hosts an annual professional tennis championship, Cleveland an annual Grand Prix, and Akron a major PGA tour event. In addition to the powerhouse of Ohio State, Ohio NCAA teams with homepages are cited below, along with OHSAA teams on the web. As a bonus, check out the Ohio Golf Guide which lists and describes all public courses in Ohio.

Akron Aeros
http://www.minorleaguebaseball.com/teams/akron
Check the Eastern League schedule and standings, get directions to the ball field, link to Aeros merchandise, and other league web sites.

All-American Soap Box Derby
http://pages.prodigy.com/SOAPBOX/
Derby Downs comes to the net with this web site full of particulars on the annual youth racing program. Directors, participants, rules, even parts and price information are included.

ASHLAND UNIVERSITY ATHLETICS

http://www.ashland.edu/athletic.html

Scores and schedules for men's and women's cross-country, soccer, softball, indoor track, swimming, basketball, and more, plus information on the athletic facilities on campus.

BALDWIN WALLACE ATHLETICS

http://www.baldwinw.edu/sports/

Everything you need to know about the Yellow Jackets and Lady Yellow Jackets, including golf and wrestling teams.

BOSTON MILLS/BRANDYWINE SKI RESORT

http://www.bmbw.com/

Directions, description of slopes and facilities, ski conditions, and prices for this resort south of Cleveland.

BOWLING GREEN UNIVERSITY ATHLETICS

http://www.bgsu.edu/offices/athletics

This site hosts web pages for all 22 intercollegiate athletic teams at the university plus campus sports clubs and intramural activities. Links to athletic staff are included.

CEDARVILLE COLLEGE YELLOW JACKETS

http://www.cedarville.edu/dept/pe/index.htm

Game by game recaps, statistics, and photo galleries of team pictures and highlights make this a very useful web site. Includes links to staff and athletic affiliations plus news releases.

CINCINNATI BENGALS

http://www.nfl.com/bengals/

The National Football League does a nice job with team home pages, and this is no exception. Fans have a vast amount of information to wade through, including a complete list of Bengals draft picks, the year in review, updates on the new stadium, coaching links, and the traditional roster and team statistics.

CINCINNATI CYCLONES INTENSE HOCKEY

http://www.cyclones.fuse.net

This is a very visually appealing site, complete with e-mail access to players, roster list, recent press releases, and game results.

CINCINNATI REDS

http://wwwmajorleaguebaseball.com/nl/cin

Batting and pitching reports, club schedule, franchise history, complete roster, plus links to minor league affiliates. Check highlights of the latest game played, and link to special featured stories.

CINCYGOLF

http://www.cincygolf.com

Listings for over 100 area golf courses, tournament schedules, online pro shops, golf bulletin board, plus links to other golf sites.

CLEAR FORK SKI AREA

http://www.richnet.net/cfslope/frameC.html

Map, calendar of events, rates and information for this ski area in Butler, Ohio.

CLEVELAND CAVALIERS

http://www.nba.com/cavs

This visually powerful site is loaded with everything for the professional basketball fan from team statistics, player profiles, schedules and scores, to information about the Gund arena and an online NBA store. Recaps of the previous game, articles about the team, plus e-mail links to the Cavs coach are all online.

CLEVELAND CRUNCH

http://www.acci.com/crunch/

Ticket info, player bios, online souvenir shopping, plus instructions on how to join the booster club of this professional soccer team.

CLEVELAND ECLIPSE

http://lawwww.cwru.edu/~eclipse

In addition to the team's soccer match schedule, roster, statistics, and ticket information, this site lists clinics offered locally by the team, plus information about the Eclipse Booster Club.

CLEVELAND GRAND PRIX

http://www.grandprix.com/events/cleveland/

Ticket information including discount opportunities, directions to the race, schedule of events, and special activities planned around the event.

CLEVELAND INDIANS

http://www.indians.com

Take a virtual tour of Jacobs Field, check ticket availability, read about recent trades and salary deals, plus team statistics, player profiles, and a virtual team shop.

CLEVELAND LIVE HIGH SCHOOL BASEBALL

http://www.cleveland.com/sports/hs/baseball

Complete schedule and roster for each Cleveland area high school baseball team, plus scouting reports, players of the week, all-stars, up to the minute game results, and a chance for you to nominate your favorite player for an MVP.

CLEVELAND LUMBERJACKS

http://www.jackshockey.com

This gorgeous site offers "rink links" to National and International Hockey League sites, "jack news," plus an invitation for fans to skate with the players after each Friday night home game. Meet the team online, schedule Buzz the mascot for a personal appearance, and best of all, hear the play by play of the Goal of the Year.

CLEVELAND ROCKERS

http://www.wnba.com/rockers

Women's professional basketball comes to Cleveland. Check out this team website loaded with highlights of previous games, team statistics, schedule and scores, plus a player profile for each woman on the roster.

CLEVELAND STATE UNIVERSITY VIKINGS

http://www.csuohio.edu/athletics

Home of the Division I NCAA wrestling tournament for 1998, this site offers information for all team sports including statistics and game schedules.

COLLEGE OF WOOSTER ATHLETICS

http://www.wooster.edu/athletics

The Scots and Lady Scots are profiled here, each team with their own page listing schedules and scores, photo galleries, and team stats. Links to athletic staff are included.

COLUMBUS CHILL

http://www.thechill.com/

This hockey team plays in Dublin. Order tickets online, read team news, check team stats, and listen to "chilling sounds" of the latest games.

COLUMBUS CLIPPERS

http://www.clippersbaseball.com

If you love baseball and live halfway between major league teams, why not become a Clippers fan? You can start by surfing their world wide web site for trivia, news stories, schedule and ticket information, then e-mail the team with comments or questions.

COLUMBUS CREW OFFICIAL WORLD WIDE WEB SITE

http://www.thecrew.com

Soccer fans will find team statistics, player photos, a season schedule, and press releases for this Columbus team.

COLUMBUS QUEST

http://www.columbusquest.com

This professional women's baseball team is a member of the American Baseball League. Its web site includes player profiles, schedule and league standings, plus press releases, ticket information, special promotions, and contact information.

DAYTONGOLF

http://www.daytongolf.com

This site is a golfer's dream. Profiles of area golf courses, including mini and indoor, area tournament schedule, calendar of events, practice facilities, teaching professionals, online pro shop — this site has it all.

DENISON UNIVERSITY BIG RED

http://www.denison.edu/athletics/varsity_page.html

Sports records and stats, current rosters and sports news for 22 varsity teams.

GOLF OHIO

http://www.golfohio.com

This commercial site is an advertising area for Ohio golf courses. Included are links to web sites of the larger golf courses in Ohio.

GREAT OHIO BICYCLE ADVENTURE

http://www.on2morning.com/cop/goba.html

Dates and route for the annual bicycle event in the Columbus area, plus quotes and pictures from past events.

KENT STATE GOLDEN FLASHES

http://www.kent.edu/athletics/

Individual pages for each of 15 women's and men's teams with statistics, rosters, schedules and weekly news releases for each, plus ticket information and a staff directory online.

LITTLE BROWN JUG WEB SITE

http://www.littlebrownjug.com

Harness racing in Delaware County. Order tickets, check upcoming events, and link to other local events from this web site.

MERCEDES SUPER 9 TENNIS TOURNAMENT

http://www.atp-cincinnati.com/

A premiere professional tournament held annually north of Cincinnati, this web site profiles participants, last year's results, this year's predictions, plus schedule, ticket prices, availability, and seating arrangements.

MIAMI UNIVERSITY REDSKINS

http://www.muohio.edu/sportsreport/

Weekly results, summaries and highlights from recent games, plus weekly and yearly sport schedules.

MID-OHIO SPORTS CAR COURSE

http://www.midohio.com

In addition to the racing season schedule, track facts and map, news releases, and souvenir information, fans can find links to camping information and other amenities they might need while visiting this race track near Dublin.

MOUNTAIN BIKING OHIO

http://www.single-track.com

Want to know where to take your mountain bike? This site tells you where the trails are, links you to people you can ride with, lets you check the weather before you leave, and provides links to classifieds where you can buy and sell your gear.

MUSKINGUM COLLEGE FIGHTING MUSKIES

http://www.muskingum.edu/~sports/

Pages for each team sport lists rosters, individual coach contacts, and team pictures. News reports and an online athletic directory are included.

OBERLIN COLLEGE ATHLETICS

http://www.oberlin.edu/~athletic/

This is a classy site — you'll love the graphics. Schedules and scores, team information including opponents, photos, and coach contacts, plus a link from each team's page to online admission information.

OHIO GOLF GUIDE

http://pathfinder.com/@@AyC9wYAZ@WPZ2bu/travel/golf/OHGOLF.HTM

This is a long URL to enter, but it's well worth it. Here you will find descriptions of all public and private courses by city, reservation policies, number of holes, greens fees for both weekend and weekdays, phone numbers, and addresses.

OHIO HIGH SCHOOL ATHLETIC ASSOCIATION (OHSAA)

http://www.ohsaa.org

Browse a member schools directory with links to school home pages, get the latest sports results, tournament information, and find out about officiating. On-line OHSAA manuals are available for downloading.

OHIO NORTHERN UNIVERSITY POLAR BEARS

http://www.onu.edu/user/fs/tglon/index.html

The Polar Bears come alive on this gorgeous web site full of information on team sports for fall, winter, and spring. School records, season previews and results are included, plus a special section called "this week in sports."

OHIO SKI DOME

http://oak-web.washington-ch.oh.us/skitrac/skiing.html

What? You've never heard of an indoor ski dome? Well, bookmark this site for updates on the longest ski slope in the world coming to Ohio for year-round skiing. Choose from three videos to see just how this project will work.

OHIO STATE BUCKEYES

http://www.ohiostatebuckeyes.com

As sophisticated as most professional sites, this is just what Buckeyes fans are looking for. Shop online for Buckeye books, join the Buckeye Club, enter the Buckeye online discussion room, or link to a myriad of sites including OSU marching band, Buckeye songs, and the OSU Sports Hall of Fame. Ticket prices and availability are online, as are featured articles about the Buckeyes, the OSU stadium, and other campus athletic facilities. Go Bucks!

OHIO UNIVERSITY BOBCATS

http://www.ohiou.edu/about/athletics/index.html

If the Bobcats are playing, you can listen online, or meet the team through player profile pages, check schedules and results, or read about athletic facilities on campus. Aspiring Bobcats can find summer camp information here as well.

OHIO WESLEYAN UNIVERSITY BATTLING BISHOPS

http://www.owu.edu/~athlweb/index.html

News releases, profiles of sports by season, plus e-mail contacts for further questions or comments. Links to other sports-related sites are included.

OTTERBEIN COLLEGE ATHLETICS

http://www.otterbein.edu/student/athletic.htm

Facts about each intercollegiate sport and all intramural activities, plus team schedules.

RUN CLEVELAND

http://www.geocities.com/Colosseum/Track/1121/

Places to run, running clubs, running stores, and scheduled races in the Cleveland area.

SNOW TRAILS SKI RESORT

http://www.snowtrails.com/frmain.htm

Season pass sales, live camera shots, interactive trails and maps, plus updated information on slope conditions for this resort near Mansfield.

THISTLEDOWN RACE TRACK

http://www.thistledown.com/

Visit this site for a behind the scenes look at the horses and track statistics.

TOLEDO MUD HENS

http://www.mudhens.com

Online ticket ordering, souvenir store, schedule information, team history, statistics and player profiles for this professional baseball team, plus a Mud Hens photo gallery, e-mail link to the team, and links to other cool web sites.

TOLEDO STORM

http://www.thestorm.com

This is a well-developed web site, with links to a complete roster including player profiles and photos, audio and video clips of Storm hockey, tickets, schedule and directional information, plus updated statistics, standings, and press releases. E-mail anyone within the Storm organization from this web page, and shop for Storm souvenirs.

UNIVERSITY OF AKRON ZIPS

http://www.akron.edu/athletics/

UNIVERSITY OF CINCINNATI BEARCATS

http://www.uc.edu/www/bearcats

A super cool pop-up menu links to each intercollegiate sport's home page where you can see athlete profiles, an overview of each program, news headlines, schedules, game results, and coaching staff links. Information on UCATS, a scholarship fund for UC athletes, is online, as are links to other teams in this conference.

UNIVERSITY OF DAYTON FLYERS

http://www.udayton.edu/athletics

Headlines, individual sports pages, and a staff directory highlight this university site.

UNIVERSITY OF TOLEDO ROCKETS

http://www.utoledo.edu/athletics

All 19 varsity sports, including 10 women's teams, are highlighted, with schedules, team statistics, game results, rosters, and press releases for each sport, plus player profiles complete with individual statistics.

WITTENBERG UNIVERSITY TIGERS

http://www.wittenberg.edu/news/athletics

Download the Wittenberg fight song, read press releases, check conference standings, visit varsity team home pages, or link to other sports Internet sites.

WRIGHT STATE UNIVERSITY RAIDERS

http://www.wright.edu/athletics

Join the Wright State listserv for fans, check on the basketball school for youth, or get ticket information, weekly sports updates, and campus recreation information.

XAVIER UNIVERSITY MUSKETEERS

http://www.xu.edu/athletics

Directions to events, ticket information, and staff directory, plus "meet the team" for each sport, and an online athletic hall of fame.

XOGGZ PROFESSIONAL SOCCER

http://lawwww.cwru.edu/~xoggz

This Columbus team's home page provides fans with news about upcoming matches, players, schedule, and ticket information. Photos, team statistics, and season results are also included, as are links to other soccer related sites.

YOUNGSTOWN STATE UNIVERSITY ATHLETICS

http://www.ysu.edu/textver/sports/athindex.htm

Simple but effective, this site lists team rosters, schedules, and e-mail addresses of each department.

VI. Family Fun

If you're looking for a great time the whole family can share check out these web sites for Ohio amusement parks, fairs, zoos and ice rinks, plus links to Disney's "family.com" featuring an interactive family activity calendar for different regions of the state. Get parenting tips, download recipes, and chat with families that share your interests.

ABUNDANCE ACROSS AMERICA

http://www.peak.org/~aaa/ohio.htm

If you believe the best part of festivals is the food they serve, this site is for you. This site lists food-related events all across the state January through December plus the recipes that make them so popular.

AIRSHOW OHIO

http://aeroweb.brooklyn.cuny.edu/

If you think the only airshows are in Cleveland and Dayton, you're wrong. Flying enthusiasts are treated to many shows in our state annually and this site will tell you when and where.

ALL ABOUT KIDS

http://www.family.com/Local/aakd/

Wondering what to do with the family in the Cincinnati area? Click on the calendar to find out what special events are planned for the upcoming month. Link to schools, read articles on parenting, enter the chat room, or join in some online activities.

BUCKEYE CENTRAL SCENIC RAILROAD

http://www.infinet.com/~pcaravan/railroad/bchome.html

Travel back in time to when the rails were a major form of passenger transportation. A history of the railroad, schedule, map and photo gallery are all part of this web site, as well as charter information for your club or organization.

CEDAR POINT

http://www.cedarpoint.com/

Did you know that Cedar Point is the world's largest amusement ride park? This site gives you close-ups on the major rides, highlights the newest attractions, and provides local accommodation and ticket price information. And before you go, e-mail for a brochure, or shop the online Cedar Point webstore.

CLEVELAND/AKRON FAMILY

http://www.family.com/Local/clev

There's lots to do for families in the Cleveland/Akron area, no matter what time of year it is. Click any day on the calendar, and this web site will provide you with choices the whole family will enjoy. And if you must stay in, you can still read parenting articles, download great family recipes, or meet other families in the chat room.

CLEVELAND METROPARKS ZOO

http://www.clemetzoo.com/

Meet Gina and Wyatt, Reba, LP, and Wildly, and learn about their new home at Wolf Wilderness. See pictures of the Rainforest, read about the zoo's research, or visit the children's web page for "fun online." Hours and admission prices plus directions to the zoo are included.

CLEVELAND NATIONAL AIR SHOW

http://www.webohio.com/airshow.html

Order tickets by mail, read about Cleveland's aviation history, and download photos of major attractions like the Blue Angels and Air Force Thunderbirds.

COSI: OHIO'S CENTER OF SCIENCE AND INDUSTRY

http://cosi.org

COSI Toledo

http://www.nbc24.com/cosi1.html

This interactive science center for all ages includes a description of major themed exhibits, including Water Works, Science Park, and Whiz Bang. Descriptions of youth programs including onsite camps and traveling school programs are included.

Cincinnati Zoo and Botanical Garden

http://www.cincyzoo.org

So much more than hours and location, this site highlights the zoo's mission — conservation and education, as well as family adventure. The zoo's Exotic Travel Program is described, as are the educational programs available through the zoo. For kids there is an online animal guessing game.

General Cinema Theatres

http://www.gctheatres.com/ohio.htm

No matter where you live, you can find out what's playing at your local GC theatre via the net. Just select theatre location, and a complete list of movies and show times appear.

Great Lakes Science Center

http://www.greatscience.com

If you've got QuickTime for windows you can download a trailer for Omnimax theatre features shown at the center. If you're an educator, you can review the tremendous science programs awaiting your students. While you're here, test your science knowledge and take the latest "pop quiz."

INVENTURE PLACE

http://www.invent.org

The National Inventors Hall of Fame is much more than a collection of exhibits honoring famous inventors. Inventure place is designed to be a "laboratory where you can explore your curiosity and creativity." Selected exhibits complete with audioclips are available at this web site, along with an online index of inventions and inventor biographies, ideal for home reference.

MAHONING VALLEY PARENT

http://www.family.com/Local/maho

Click on the calendar and this Disney site will list what family events are scheduled in the Youngstown area. Link to schools, parenting articles, online activities, and other family sites.

NASA LEWIS VISITOR CENTER

http://www.lerc.nasa.gov/WWW/PAO/html/visitlew.htm

If you're interested in space, you'll find a wealth of information at this site. View the Apollo Command module, moon rocks, witness space shuttle launches, link to updates on current NASA missions. Read detailed explanations of mission objectives and findings, plus crew biographies. Check the schedule for visiting lectures at the center, plus see what's available through the outreach and traveling exhibits program.

OHIO COUNTY FAIRS

http://www.state.oh.us/agr/

Find out the schedule for this year's county fairs.

OHIO EXPO CENTER

http://www.ohioexpocenter.com/

Find out what's happening this month at this large indoor event showplace in Columbus.

OHIO STATE FAIR

http://www.ohioexpocenter.com/

Schedules, maps, and promotions for the largest annual agricultural fair in Ohio.

PIONEER WATER-LAND

http://www.virtcity.com/business/waterland

This waterpark near Chardon lists activities, hours, admission and contact information.

PREHISTORIC FOREST

http://www.mysteryhill.com

Think your kids would like to dig for bones and fossils, or see fifteen life-size dinosaurs? Then check this web site for hours, admission fees and a map to this entertainment site near Marblehead.

RITTER PLANETARIUM AND BROOKS OBSERVATORY

http://www.physics.utoledo.edu/~rpbo/

If our mission to Mars has your family interested in the planets, visit this web site for information about public and school programs plus astronomy exhibits at this planetarium near Toledo.

SEA WORLD

http://www.bev.net/education/SeaWorld/homepage.html

Before you make the trip to Aurora, preview the fun that's in store. The whole family can learn about sea life from this educationally oriented page, and teachers can download curriculum guides. For budding oceanographers and marine biologists, information about Sea World Adventure camps is included.

TOLEDO PARENT

http://www.family.com/Local/tole/

Feature articles, school links, family travel advice, online activities, and best of all an interactive calendar of events for families in the Toledo area.

TOLEDO ZOO

http://www.toledozoo.org/

Zoo web sites are so educational. Even if you can't get to Toledo, stop by this site for a cybertour with Safari Sam. He'll show you photos of zoo residents and tell you all about them. If you can get to Toledo, check the hours, location, and admission fees here before you go.

WINTERHURST ICE RINK

http://www.lkwdpl.org/city/skate.htm

This huge rink located in Lakewood is open year-round and boasts quite a large web site full of information on the facility, programs, hours, and rink rentals. There are links to pages about outstanding skaters who have trained at Winterhurst, including Olympic gold medal winners. Local high school hockey teams post their schedules here.

VII. Education

Whether you're shopping for a school district in Ohio, or you're already firmly planted, you'll find this collection of web sites a real eye-opener to the state of education in Ohio. From elementary school to research university, these pages provide a wealth of statistics and detail, not only about the institutions, but about the broader community of learning.

MAJOR SITES

WEB 66

http://web66.coled.umn.edu/schools/US/Ohio.html
An "International WWW School Registry" put out by the University of Minnesota, this site provides links to over 250 elementary, middle, and secondary schools, public school districts, and Ohio educational organizations. While far from comprehensive, it is a good starting point for taking a look at Ohio schools on the web.

OHIO DEPARTMENT OF EDUCATION

http://www.ode.ohio.gov/
True to any government site, this is where the statistics are. Student-pupil ratios, teacher salaries, proficiency test scores—every statistic you need from the public school system.

Ohio Public School Districts

School sports schedules, homework assignments, school calendars, lunch menus, special projects, and class news, plus links to state and national educational sites and homework help. From these district home pages, link to individual pages for each elementary, middle and secondary school. For an outstanding example of what the Internet can do for local education, take a look at the Lakewood City Schools home page linking libraries, schools and community. Students regularly do their homework online at the public library, the school, or from home and are provided through a joint community effort with both technology and personal guidance.

Akron Public Schools
http://www.summit.k12.oh.us/site/district/akron/akron.htm

Alliance City Schools, Alliance, Ohio
http://www.aviators.stark.k12.oh.us

Anthony Wayne Local Schools, Whitehouse, Ohio
http://198.234.116.31/

Arlington Local Schools, Arlington, Ohio
http://www.noacsc.ohio.gov/hancock/ag/

Austintown Local Schools, Austintown, Ohio
http://www.cisnet.com.fitch/

BARBERTON CITY SCHOOLS
http://www.summit.k12.oh.us/site/district/barberton/barberton.htm

BATH LOCAL SCHOOLS, LIMA, OHIO
http://www.noacsc.ohio.gov/allen/ba/

BEACHWOOD SCHOOLS, BEACHWOOD, OHIO
http://mail.bw.lgca.ohio.gov/

BEAVER LOCAL SCHOOLS, LISBON, OHIO
http://www.access.ohio.gov/beav/beav.htm

BOARDMAN LOCAL SCHOOLS, BOARDMAN, OHIO
http://www.cisnet.com/bhs/

CAMPBELL CITY SCHOOLS, CAMPBELL, OHIO
http://www.access.ohio.gov/camp/camp.htm

CANFIELD LOCAL SCHOOLS, CANFIELD, OHIO
http://www.access.ohio.gov/canfield/canf.htm

CANTON CITY SCHOOLS, CANTON, OHIO
http://www.canton-ohio.com/ccs/ccshome.html

CANTON LOCAL SCHOOLS, CANTON, OHIO
http://maccat.stark.k12.oh.us/

CARDINGTON-LINCOLN LOCAL SCHOOLS, CARDINGTON, OHIO
http://www.treca.ohio.gov/schools/card/cardington.html/

CHARDON SCHOOLS, CHARDON, OHIO

http://www.lgca.ohio.gov/districts/Chardon/

CHESAPEAKE SCHOOLS, CHESAPEAKE, OHIO

http://peakeweb.scoca.ohio.gov/

CINCINNATI PUBLIC SCHOOLS, CINCINNATI, OHIO

http://cps.cin.ix.net

**CLEVELAND HEIGHTS-UNIVERSITY HEIGHTS SCHOOLS,
CLEVELAND HEIGHTS, OHIO**

http://tiger.chuh.cleveland-heights.k12.oh.us/

CLINTON-MASSIE LOCAL SCHOOLS, CLARKSVILLE, OHIO

http://198.234.208.7/

COPLEY/FAIRLAWN CITY SCHOOLS

http://www.summit.k12.oh.us/site/district/copley/copley.htm

COLUMBUS PUBLIC SCHOOLS, COLUMBUS, OHIO

http://www.columbus.k12.oh.us/

COLUMBIANA EXEMPTED VILLAGE SCHOOLS, COLUMBIANA, OHIO

http://www.access.ohio.gov/columbiana/clip.html

COVENTRY LOCAL SCHOOLS

http://www.summit.k12.oh.us/site/district/coventry/coventry.htm

CROOKSVILLE EXEMPTED SCHOOLS, CROOKSVILLE, OHIO

http://www.seorf.ohiou.edu/~xx045/hide/davidp/chs/cville.htm

CUYAHOGA FALLS CITY SCHOOLS

http://www.summit.k12.oh.us/cuyahogafalls/

DAYTON SCHOOLS, DAYTON, OHIO

http://www.dayton.net/edu/

DUBLIN CITY SCHOOLS, DUBLIN, OHIO

http://www.dublin.k12.oh.us/

EAST LIVERPOOL CITY SCHOOLS, EAST LIVERPOOL, OHIO

http://www.access.ohio.gov/east/home.htm

EASTERN LOCAL SCHOOL DISTRICT, REEDSVILLE, OHIO

http://www.seorf.ohiou.edu/~xx048

FAIRFIELD CITY SCHOOLS, FAIRFIELD, OHIO

http://www.iac.net/~fairfld/

FAIRLESS LOCAL SCHOOLS, NAVARRE, OHIO

http://fairless.stark.k12.oh.us/

FREDERICKTOWN LOCAL SCHOOLS, FREDERICKTOWN, OHIO

http://www.knox.net/knox/schools/fredtown/

GAHANNA-JEFFERSON PUBLIC SCHOOLS, GAHANNA, OHIO

http://www.gahanna.k12.oh.us/

GREEN SCHOOL DISTRICT

http://www.summit.k12.oh.us/site/district/green/index.html

HOLGATE LOCAL SCHOOLS, HOLGATE, OHIO

http://www.nwoca.ohio.gov/www/sites/holgate/holgate.html

HUDSON LOCAL SCHOOL DISTRICT, HUDSON, OHIO

http://www.hudson.edu/

HUNTINGTON LOCAL SCHOOLS, CHILLICOTHE, OHIO

http://198.234.186.241/huntington/default/htm

INDEPENDENCE LOCAL SCHOOLS, INDEPENDENCE, OHIO

http://www.cyberdrive.net/independence/

INDIAN HILL SCHOOL DISTRICT, CINCINNATI, OHIO

http://www.ih.k12.oh.us/

IRONTON CITY SCHOOLS, IRONTON, OHIO

http://www.tigertown.com/

JACKSON CENTER LOCAL SCHOOLS, JACKSON CENTER, OHIO

http://schools.woco.ohio.gov/JC/

JACKSON LOCAL SCHOOLS, MASSILLON, OHIO

http://jackson.stark.k12.oh.us/

KENSTON SCHOOLS, KENSTON, OHIO

http://www.kenston.k12.oh.us/

KETTERING-MORAINE SCHOOLS, KETTERING, OHIO

http://156.63.162.3/

KIRTLAND SCHOOLS, KIRTLAND, OHIO

http://www.kirtland.k12.ohio.us/

LAKE LOCAL SCHOOLS, UNIONTOWN, OHIO

http://www.powerpages.net/lake/lakeschools.htm

LAKEWOOD CITY SCHOOLS, LAKEWOOD, OHIO

http://www.lkwdpl.org/schools/

LEETONIA EXEMPTED VILLAGE SCHOOLS, LEETONIA, OHIO

http://www.access.ohio.gov/leet/leet.htm

LOUISVILLE CITY SCHOOLS, LOUISVILLE, OHIO

http://leopard.stark.k12.oh.us/

LOVELAND CITY SCHOOLS, LOVELAND, OHIO

http://www.loveland.k12.oh.us/

MADISON SCHOOLS, MADISON, OHIO

http://www.ncocc.ohio.gov/madison/

MAHONING VALLEY JOINT VOCATIONAL SCHOOLS

http://access-k12.org/mjvs/mjvs.htm

MANCHESTER LOCAL SCHOOLS

http://www.summit.k12.oh.us/site/district/manchester/manchester.htm

MARIETTA CITY SCHOOLS, MARIETTA, OHIO

http://mcnet.marietta.edu/~mcs/

MARION CITY SCHOOLS, MARION, OHIO

http://mac21.treca.ohio.gov/

MARLINGTON LOCAL SCHOOLS, ALLIANCE, OHIO

http://dukes.stark.k12.oh.us/

MASSILLON CITY SCHOOLS, MASSILLON, OHIO

http://tigerweb.stark.k12.oh.us/

McDonald Local Schools, McDonald, Ohio
http://www.mcdonald.k12.oh.us/

Miami County Schools, Troy, Ohio
http://www.erinet.com/troy/schools.html

Miami Trace Schools, Washington Court House, Ohio
http://oak-web.oak-web.washington-ch.oh.us/mt/

Middletown City Schools, Middletown, Ohio
http://www.mcsd.k12.oh.us/

Minerva Local Schools, Minerva, Ohio
http://lion.stark.k12.oh.us/

Mogodore Local Schools
http://www.summit.k12.oh.us/site/district/mogadore/mogadore.htm

Montpelier Exempted Village Schools, Montpelier, Ohio
http://www.montpelier.k12.oh.us

Nordonia Hills City Schools
http://www.summit.k12.oh.us/site/district/nordonia/nordonia.htm

North Canton City Schools, North Canton, Ohio
http://viking.stark.k12.oh.us/

North Olmsted City Schools, North Olmsted, Ohio
http://nolms.leeca.ohio.gov/nocs

Northwest Local Schools, Canal Fulton, Ohio
http://piglet.stark.k12.oh.us/

NORTON CITY SCHOOLS

http://www.summit.k12.oh.us/site/district/norton/norton.htm

OAKWOOD CITY SCHOOLS, OAKWOOD, OHIO

http://www.oakwood.k12.oh.us/

OLMSTED FALLS CITY SCHOOLS, OLMSTED FALLS, OHIO

http://www.leeca.esu.k12.oh.us/ofcs/ofcs.html

ORANGE CITY SCHOOLS, PEPPER PIKE, OHIO

http://www.orangeschools.org/

OSNABURG LOCAL SCHOOLS, EAST CANTON, OHIO

http://ecweb.stark.k12.oh.us/

PAINESVILLE CITY SCHOOLS

http://156.63.242.18/

PERRY LOCAL SCHOOLS, MASSILLON, OHIO

http://perrynet.stark.k12.oh.us/

PERRY LOCAL SCHOOLS, PERRY, OHIO

http://www.perryschools.lgca.ohio.gov

PLAIN LOCAL SCHOOL DISTRICT, CANTON, OHIO

http://www.eagle.stark.k12.oh.us/

POLAND LOCAL SCHOOLS, POLAND, OHIO

http://www.neont.com/pshs/index.htm

PORTSMOUTH CITY SCHOOLS, PORTSMOUTH, OHIO

http://portsweb.scoca.ohio.gov/

SALEM CITY SCHOOLS, SALEM, OHIO

http://www.access.ohio.gov/sale/index.htm

SANDY VALLEY LOCAL SCHOOLS, SANDY VALLEY, OHIO

http://cardweb.stark.k12.oh.us/

SEBRING LOCAL SCHOOLS, SEBRING, OHIO

http://www.access.ohio.gov/sebring/sebr.htm

SHADYSIDE LOCAL SCHOOLS, SHADYSIDE, OHIO

http://www.shadyside.k12.oh.us/

SHAKER HEIGHTS CITY SCHOOLS, SHAKER HEIGHTS, OHIO

http://www.shaker.k12.oh.us/

SOUTH POINT LOCAL SCHOOLS, SOUTH POINT, OHIO

http://pointnet.scoca.ohio.gov/public/default.htm

SOUTH RANGE LOCAL SCHOOLS, NORTH LIMA, OHIO

http://www.access.ohio.gov/sran/sran.htm

STEUBENVILLE CITY SCHOOLS, STEUBENVILLE, OHIO

http://www.weir.net/~pbasil/

STOW-MONROE FALLS CITY SCHOOLS

http://www.summit.k12.oh.us/site/district/stow.stow.htm

STRYKER LOCAL SCHOOLS

http://www.nwoca.ohio.gov/~stryker_www/

SYLVANIA SCHOOL DISTRICT, SYLVANIA, OHIO

http://206.98.19.1/sylvania/schools/main.htm

TALLMADGE CITY SCHOOLS
http://www.summit.k12.oh.us/site/district/tallmadge/tallmadge.htm

TRIMBLE LOCAL SCHOOLS
http://www.seorf.ohiou.edu/~xx045/hide/kendrac/tls/tlshpg.htm

TWINSBURG CITY SCHOOLS
http://www.summit.k12.oh.us/site/district/twinsburg/twinsburg.htm

UPPER ARLINGTON SCHOOLS, UPPER ARLINGTON, OHIO
http://www.upper-arlington.k12.oh.us/

URBANA CITY SCHOOLS, URBANA, OHIO
http://schools.woco.ohio.gov/Urbana/

WAYNESFIELD-GOSHEN LOCAL SCHOOLS, WAYNESVILLE, OHIO
http://schools.woco.ohio.gov/wg/

WEST BRANCH LOCAL SCHOOLS, BELOIT, OHIO
http://www.access.ohio.gov/branch/wbra.htm

WEST CLERMONT SCHOOLS, CINCINNATI, OHIO
http://www.westcler.k12.oh.us/

WESTERVILLE CITY SCHOOLS, WESTERVILLE, OHIO
http://www.westerville.k12.oh.us/

WILLOUGHBY-EASTLAKE CITY SCHOOLS, WILLOUGHBY, OHIO
http://www.lgca.oh.gov/districts/willoughby-eastlake/

WOODMORE LOCAL SCHOOLS, WOODVILLE, OHIO
http://www.woodmore.k12.oh.us/

Woodridge Local Schools
http://www.summit.k12.oh.us/site/district/woodridge/woodridge.htm

Wooster City Schools, Wooster, Ohio
http://www.wooster.k12.oh.us/

Zanesville City Schools, Zanesville, Ohio
http://www.zanesville.k12.oh.us/

Private Schools

Cincinnati Country Day School
http://www.ccds.cincinnati.oh.us/

Cleveland School of the Arts
http://www.lerc.nasa.gov/www/k-12/csa/csa.html

Columbus Academy
http://ca131.ca-net.pvt.k12.oh.us/

Columbus Diocesan Department of Education
http://www.cd.pvt.k12.oh.us

Diocese of Cleveland Office of Catholic Education
http://www.oce.org/

Gilmour Academy, Gates Mills, Ohio
http://gilmour.pvt.k12.oh.us/

HAWKEN SCHOOL, LYNDHURST, OHIO

http://www.hawken.edu/

MAUMEE VALLEY COUNTRY DAY SCHOOL, TOLEDO, OHIO

http://www.mvcds.com/

MAYERSON ACADEMY, CINCINNATI, OHIO

http://www.mayacad.org/

UNIVERSITY SCHOOL, SHAKER HEIGHTS, OHIO

http://www.us.edu/

WELLINGTON SCHOOL, COLUMBUS, OHIO

http://www.wellington.org/

WESTERN RESERVE ACADEMY, HUDSON, OHIO

http://wra-reserve.org

EDUCATIONAL ORGANIZATIONS AND RESOURCES

Teachers and parents alike will find great curriculum support ideas, statistics, and administrative links among these sites.

LIVING OHIO GOVERNMENT SERIES
http://www.logs.org/
A wonderful page intended for educators, this site discusses the process of Ohio government, links to free materials, museums, and other resources. The "Factoids" section highlights several impressive school projects concerning local history. Great information for students.

NORTHEAST OHIO SPECIAL EDUCATION REGIONAL RESOURCE CENTER
http://www.access.ohio.gov/neoserrc/serrc000.htm
Serving Ashtabula, Mahoning, and Trumbull counties, this site describes its purpose and programs, plus links to its mother site, the Ohio SERRC Network.

OHIO ASSOCIATION OF ELEMENTARY SCHOOL ADMINISTRATORS
http://www.oaesa.org/home.htm
Direct e-mail links for answers on administrative, legislative, and membership questions.

OHIO BOARD OF REGENTS
http://www.bor.ohio.gov/
The planning and coordinating agency for higher education in Ohio provides a site describing its mission and programs plus a comprehensive list of colleges and universities in Ohio with links to the web page of each.

OHIO COUNCIL FOR THE SOCIAL STUDIES

http://www.iac.net/~pfilio/

With links to hot social studies sites, professional organizations and listservs for educators, this web site is a great asset to the teaching profession. Includes National Standards for the Social Studies plus the Ohio State Model: Social Studies.

OHIO EDUCATION ASSOCIATION

http://www.oea.columbus.oh.us/index.html

Links to education in the news, educational policies, professional development, plus the Online Educator, a site featuring free lesson plans, listservs for educators, and educational "hot links."

OHIO SCHOOLNET

http://www.ohioschoolnet.k12.oh.us/

In case you haven't heard, this five-year program established in 1994 by the Ohio state government is attempting to network Ohio's public school classrooms by providing wiring and equipment. This wonderful web sites provides visitors with the vision and success stories behind the program, plus great links to web sites and resources for teachers, parents and students.

PUTNAM VALLEY'S EDUCATIONAL STANDARDS LINKS

http://putwest.boces.org/StSt/Ohio.html/

The latest edition of the Standards for Ohio Schools plus its discussion guide is available online from this site.

SCIENCE EDUCATION ENHANCING THE DEVELOPMENT OF SKILLS (SEEDS)

http://seedsnet.stark.k12.oh.us

In an effort to increase science proficiency starting in the elementary grades, a group of teachers in Stark County with help from the National Science Foundation developed this terrific web site. Units for elementary science curriculum are available online for "hands-on, minds-on" learning. If you're a science teacher or homeschooler, don't miss this gift from your peers.

SOUTHWEST OHIO COUNCIL FOR THE SOCIAL STUDIES

http://www.iac.net/~pfilio/

STARKNET EDUCATION NETWORK

http://www.stark.k12.oh.us/

If you're an educator in Stark County, bookmark this page. Continuing education opportunities and graduate credit class locations, course calendar for the Teacher Technology Center, Stark County school calendars, plus online registration for classes are all provided. Link to search engines, get on the StarkNet news server, link to the Repository or get Ohio Proficiency Test results.

SUMMIT COUNTY EDUCATIONAL SERVICE CENTER

http://www.summit.k12.oh.us/

This educational center and web site host for the Summit County school systems has a wonderful web page with links to sites for teachers and parents, a calendar for the technology lab, and the home pages for all the school districts within the county.

TUITION TRUST AUTHORITY
http://www.prepaid-tuition.state.oh.us/
Designed to help Ohio citizens save for their children's college education, this state government link tells the background of the program and how to enroll.

OHIO HOMESCHOOL RESOURCES

Even if you don't homeschool, these sites are full of great ideas to keep kids learning.

ADVENTURES IN HOMESCHOOLING
http://www.homerc.com/

CHRISTIAN HOME EDUCATORS OF OHIO
http://www.home-school.com/Groups/OhioCHEO.html

COLUMBUS AREA HOMESCHOOLING INFORMATION
http://www.infinet.com/~baugust/ohio.html

GREATER CINCINNATI HOME SCHOOLERS
http://w3.goodnews.net/~herronrj/

HOME EDUCATION LEAGUE OF PARENTS- CENTRAL OHIO
http://www.redbird.net/Clark/helpco.html

HOMESCHOOLING IN OHIO
http://members.stratus.net/thorn/school.html

OHIO COLLEGES AND UNIVERSITIES

With the advent of the world wide web it has now become possible to virtually tour any Ohio campus, check course catalogs, and apply for admission, all from your personal computer. Some institutions even offer courses over the net. Every site has community links and special features of its own — the best are noted. For library catalog web sites, see the "Ohio Libraries" chapter.

AIR FORCE INSTITUTE OF TECHNOLOGY
http://www.afit.af.mil/

ANTIOCH COLLEGE
http://antioch-college.edu/

ART ACADEMY OF CINCINNATI
http://www2.eos.net/artacady/
Check out the online gallery.

ASHLAND UNIVERSITY
http://www.ashland.edu/

BALDWIN-WALLACE UNIVERSITY
http://www.bw.edu/
Great links to Cleveland area sites.

BLUFFTON COLLEGE
http://www.bluffton.edu/
Online employment opportunities.

BOWLING GREEN STATE UNIVERSITY
http://www.bgsu.edu/

BOWLING GREEN-FIRELANDS CAMPUS
http://www.bgsu.edu/colleges/firelands/

CAPITAL UNIVERSITY
http://www.capital.edu/
Links to Evangelical Lutheran Church in America.

CASE WESTERN UNIVERSITY
http://www.cwru.edu
Newsline contains community links to government, media, transportation, and online companies. Cleveland freenet link, bus schedule. Don't miss library catalog in "Ohio Libraries" chapter.

CEDARVILLE COLLEGE
http://www.cedarville.edu/
Christian resources plus links to Dayton and Cincinnati.

CLARK STATE COMMUNITY COLLEGE
http://www.clark.cc.oh.us/

CLEVELAND INSTITUTE OF ART
http://www.cia.edu/
List of summer workshops for area artists.

CLEVELAND INSTITUTE OF MUSIC
http://www.cwru.edu/CIM/cimhome.html

CLEVELAND STATE UNIVERSITY

http://www.csuohio.edu/

COLLEGE OF MOUNT ST. JOSEPH

http://www.msj.edu/

COLLEGE OF WOOSTER

http://www.wooster.edu/

COLUMBUS COLLEGE OF ART AND DESIGN

http://www.ccad.edu/

COLUMBUS STATE COMMUNITY COLLEGE

http://www.colstate.cc.oh.us/docs/cscc.htm

CUYAHOGA COMMUNITY COLLEGE

http://www.tri-c.cc.oh.us/
Campus job openings online.

DAVID N. MYERS COLLEGE

http://ellen.dnmyers.edu/
*College Options Online (COOL) — external independent
study by www and e-mail.*

DEFIANCE COLLEGE

http://www.defiance.edu/

DENISON UNIVERSITY

http://www.denison.edu/

DEVRY INSTITUTE OF TECHNOLOGY

http://www.devrycols.edu/

EDISON STATE COMMUNITY COLLEGE

http://www.edison.cc.oh.us/

FRANCISCAN UNIVERSITY OF STEUBENVILLE

http://www.franuniv.edu/
Catholic Resources page.

FRANKLIN UNIVERSITY

http://www.franklin.edu/

HEIDELBERG COLLEGE

http://www.heidelberg.edu/
Link to Fallen Timbers Archaeology site and water quality lab.

HIRAM COLLEGE

http://www.hiram.edu/

HOCKING TECHNICAL COLLEGE

http://www.hocking.cc.oh.us/

JOHN CARROLL UNIVERSITY

http://www.jcu.edu/
Outstanding Cleveland links.

KENT STATE UNIVERSITY (KSU)

http://www.kent.edu/

KSU-ASHTABULA CAMPUS

http://www.ashtabula.kent.edu/

KSU-East Liverpool Campus

http://www.kenteliv.kent.edu/

KSU-Geauga Campus

http://www.geauga.kent.edu/

KSU-Salem Campus

http://www.salem.kent.edu/

KSU-Stark Campus

http://www.stark.kent.edu/

KSU-Trumball Campus

http://www.trumball.kent.edu/

KSU-Tuscarawas Campus

http://www.tusc.kent.edu/

Kenyon College

http://www.kenyon.edu/

Lakeland Community College

http://www.lakeland.cc.oh.us/index.htm

Lima Technical College

http://www.worcnet.gen.oh.us/LTC/ltc.htm

Lorain County Community College

http://www.lorain.cc.oh.us/
Campus job listings online.

MALONE COLLEGE

http://www.malone.edu/

MARIETTA COLLEGE

http://www.marietta.edu/
Good local information.

MEDICAL COLLEGE OF OHIO AT TOLEDO

http://www.mco.edu/
Medical links ranging in topic from allied health to telemedicine.

MIAMI UNIVERSITY

http://www.muohio.edu/
Well-designed site with everything students need to know.

MIAMI UNIVERSITY-HAMILTON CAMPUS

http://www.ham.muohio.edu/

MIAMI UNIVERSITY- MIDDLETOWN CAMPUS

http://www.mid.muohio.edu/

MOUNT UNION COLLEGE

http://www.muc.edu/

MOUNT VERNON NAZARENE COLLEGE

http://www.mvnc.edu/

MUSKINGUM COLLEGE

http://www.muskingum.edu/

NORTHEASTERN OHIO UNIVERSITIES COLLEGE OF MEDICINE

http://www.neoucom.edu/

Health-related links.

NORTHWEST STATE COMMUNITY COLLEGE

http://www.nscc.cc.oh.us/

Offers college courses via the Internet.

OBERLIN COLLEGE

http://www.oberlin.edu/

OHIO COLLEGE OF PODIATRIC MEDICINE

http://www.ocpm.edu/

Links to podiatry sites nationwide.

OHIO DOMINICAN COLLEGE

http://www.odc.edu/

OHIO NORTHERN UNIVERSITY

http://www.onu.edu/

Links to drug topic sites through College of Pharmacy.

OHIO STATE UNIVERSITY

http://www.acs.ohio-state.edu/

Electronic course availability, Buckeyes home page. Each school has own home page with related links.

OHIO STATE UNIVERSITY-LIMA

http://www.lima.ohio-state.edu/

OHIO STATE UNIVERSITY-MANSFIELD

http://www.mansfield.ohio-state.edu/

OHIO STATE UNIVERSITY-MARION

http://www.marion.ohio-state.edu/

OHIO UNIVERSITY

http://www.ohiou.edu/

OHIO UNIVERSITY-CHILLICOTHE CAMPUS

http://www.cats.ohiou.edu/~childept/

OHIO UNIVERSITY-LANCASTER CAMPUS

http://www.cats.ohiou.edu/~lancdept/

OHIO UNIVERSITY-SOUTHERN CAMPUS

http://www.cats.ohiou.edu/~ousc/ousc.htm

OHIO UNIVERSITY-ZANESVILLE CAMPUS

http://www.cats.ohiou.edu/~zansdept/

OHIO WESLEYAN UNIVERSITY

http://www.owu.edu/
Links to Delaware, Ohio home page.

OTTERBEIN COLLEGE

http://www.otterbein.edu/

OWENS STATE COMMUNITY COLLEGE

http://www.owens.cc.oh.us/

SHAWNEE STATE UNIVERSITY

http://www.shawnee.edu/

SINCLAIR COMMUNITY COLLEGE

http://www.sinclair.edu/

Offers Sinclair Electronic College — courses over the Internet.

TERRA STATE COMMUNITY COLLEGE

http://www.terra.cc.oh.us/

THE UNION INSTITUTE

http://www.tui.edu/

Great virtual library.

UNIVERSITY OF AKRON

http://www.uakron.edu

UNIVERSITY OF AKRON-WAYNE

http://www.wayne.uakron.edu/

UNIVERSITY OF CINCINNATI

http://www.uc.edu/

Hosts Netwellness, a huge health database — see chapter on Health.

UNIVERSITY OF CINCINNATI-CLERMONT

http://www.clc.uc.edu/

Interesting links to Clermont County environmental sites from asbestos referral to emergency spill response hotline.

UNIVERSITY OF CINCINNATI-RAYMOND WALTERS

http://www.rwc.uc.edu/

UNIVERSITY OF DAYTON

http://www.udayton.edu/

UNIVERSITY OF FINDLAY

http://www.findlay.edu/

UNIVERSITY OF TOLEDO

http://www.utoledo.edu/

URSULINE COLLEGE

http://www.en.com/ursweb/index.htm

WALSH UNIVERSITY

http://www.walsh.edu/

WILMINGTON COLLEGE

http://www.wilmington.edu/

WITTENBERG UNIVERSITY

http://www.wittenberg.edu/

WRIGHT STATE UNIVERSITY

http://www.wright.edu/
Travel links, Ohio Magazine online, great health links.

XAVIER UNIVERSITY

http://www.xu.edu/

YOUNGSTOWN STATE UNIVERSITY

http://www.ysu.edu/

VIII. Libraries

Talk about a storehouse of local information. Any library with a home page is also a community page and with dial-up access to many large library systems, often a free ride to the Internet. Along with local library catalogs, some of the larger public library sites link to college and university catalogs along with the reference databases they support. OPLIN and OhioLINK have made Ohio libraries Internet leaders by providing the financial and technological support as well as implementing cooperative networks across the state. If you live in Ohio, you are connected.

PUBLIC LIBRARIES WITH A WEB PAGE

AKRON-SUMMIT COUNTY PUBLIC LIBRARY
http://www.neo.lrun.com/Akron_Summit_County_Public_Library/
Search the catalog online, link to branches, send e-mail to the library, and check on special services like the library delivery service to homebound patrons.

ALEXANDRIA PUBLIC LIBRARY
http://mocin.denison.edu/libraries/alex/alexhome.htm
Hours and services, plus a connection to OPLIN, but no web library catalog as of yet.

ANDOVER PUBLIC LIBRARY

http://www.andover.lib.oh.us

Community links, library policies and programs.

BELLEVUE PUBLIC LIBRARY

http://clevnet.cpl.org/bellevue

This small library has a large homepage thanks to its membership in the Clevnet library group. Patrons accessing the online catalog search the catalogs of over twenty other libraries in northern Ohio, are able to place reserves online, and may view their borrower records. This page features a direct link to OPLIN and the electronic resources page of the Cleveland Public Library.

BIRCHARD PUBLIC LIBRARY (FREMONT)

http://www.birchard.lib.oh.us/

This library offers a direct link to OPLIN, plus a description of all department services, and a calendar of events.

BLUFFTON-RICHLAND PUBLIC LIBRARY

http://library.norweld.lib.oh.us/Bluffton

History of the library, its funding sources, internet use policy, plus a link to the library's online catalog telnet connection.

BRUMBACK LIBRARY (VAN WERT)

http://206.102.94.166

Links to Trumball County officials, local schools, and cities, and useful reference information on the Internet.

CARROLL COUNTY DISTRICT LIBRARY (CARROLLTON)

http://www.molo.lib.oh.us/home/carroll/

Services offered by each department are listed, plus a map showing library location, an e-mail link to send messages directly to the library, and a list of Internet search engines you will find very useful.

CHILLICOTHE AND ROSS COUNTY PUBLIC LIBRARY

http://www.oval.lib.oh.us/ros/roshome.html

Special services include links to the Library for the Blind. A direct link to OPLIN is available from this page, as are library services and Internet policy.

CINCINNATI PUBLIC LIBRARY
(PUBLIC LIBRARY OF CINCINNATI AND HAMILTON COUNTY)

http://plch.lib.oh.us

This huge library system offers an online catalog, electronic resources, and a direct link to OPLIN. A unique and extremely useful feature for card holders is the library's online renewal system.

CLARK COUNTY PUBLIC LIBRARY (SPRINGFIELD)

http://www.ccpl.lib.oh.us

Community links include local colleges, the Springfield Art Museum, and the city of Springfield. The online catalog and OPLIN link round out a very useful library web site.

CLEVELAND HEIGHTS-UNIVERSITY HEIGHTS PUBLIC LIBRARY

http://www.chuhpl.lib.oh.us

Take a virtual tour, access OPLIN, a list of search engines, or the Clevnet catalog. Policies, services, book discussion lists, library events, and a list of magazine titles owned by the library are all online.

CLEVELAND PUBLIC LIBRARY

http://www.cpl.org

Definitely the most comprehensive and well-produced library catalog in the state, and one of the best in the country. This site is the starting point for virtually anywhere you want to go on the Internet, from local to international. Registered borrowers can access the catalog, place their own reserves, and check their patron records. Anyone dialing in or using the web page can also browse the catalog or use electronic resources grouped by library department, such as maps, science and technology, fine arts, and general reference. Included is a list of search engines and directories for those who wish to explore the web a little further.

CLYDE PUBLIC LIBRARY

http://clevnet.cpl.org/clyde

This small library gets a big boost from Clevnet membership, combining its online catalog with more than twenty others in northern Ohio. OPLIN is available from the front page, and there are links to Cleveland Public Library's electronic resources.

CONNEAUT CARNEGIE LIBRARY

http://www.nforce.com/clients/nola/conneaut/

List of services, Internet policy, and hopefully soon an online catalog.

COSHOCTON PUBLIC LIBRARY

http://www.molo.lib.oh.us/home/cosh/

Get information on dial-up access to the library catalog, see a map to the library, read a list of new materials. Internet links and search engines are included.

CUYAHOGA COUNTY PUBLIC LIBRARY

http://clio1.cuyahoga.lib.oh.us/home/index

In addition to an electronic online catalog, this page offers links to community resources and Internet resources.

DAYTON AND MONTGOMERY COUNTY PUBLIC LIBRARY

http://www.dayton.lib.oh.us

This huge library system offers an online catalog, subject access to the Internet, collection policy, and lists of hot titles.

DEFIANCE PUBLIC LIBRARY

http://www.defiance.lib.oh.us

This library offers its catalog online, along with a list of historical records kept within the library's local history department.

DOVER PUBLIC LIBRARY

http://www.molo.lib.oh.us/home/dover/

Community links, selected search engines, plus a map to the library highlight this page.

EAST CLEVELAND PUBLIC LIBRARY

http://www.ecpl.lib.oh.us

This Clevnet library has a well-developed home page linking to OPLIN, Cleveland Public Library electronic resources, and an online catalog it shares with more than twenty other northern Ohio libraries.

ELLA M. EVERHARD PUBLIC LIBRARY (WADSWORTH)

http://clevnet.cpl.org/wadsworth

A very small library system with a great web site, including an online catalog shared by over twenty other Clevnet libraries, a direct connection to OPLIN, and the electronic resources page of the Cleveland Public Library.

ELYRIA PUBLIC LIBRARY

http://clevnet.cpl.org/elyria

This site enjoys all the features of a Clevnet library web site-direct links to OPLIN, an online catalog shared by twenty other northern Ohio libraries, access to Cleveland Public Library's electronic databases, plus online reserves and patron information for library cardholders.

EUCLID PUBLIC LIBRARY

http://clevnet.cpl.org/euclid

Another Clevnet library, enjoying all the links and resources of this huge library consortium. Exploring this catalog will take awhile, but you'll get wherever you want to go.

FAIRFIELD COUNTY DISTRICT LIBRARY

http://netra.clc.lib.oh.us/fcd/

This page has good links to local sites, including Fairfield High and the local arts council. The Library Channel, a family-friendly Internet menu, is available from this site.

FAIRPORT PUBLIC LIBRARY

http://www.fairport.lib.oh.us

A Clevnet Library with all the advantages — a library catalog accessing records from over 20 northern Ohio libraries, Cleveland Public Library electronic resources, and an OPLIN link from its home page.

FINDLAY-HANCOCK COUNTY PUBLIC LIBRARY

http://www.findlay.lib.oh.us/

Genealogists will appreciate the list of local history resources.

GIRARD FREE LIBRARY

http://www.girard.lib.oh.us/

Links to community, OPLIN, search engines, and library events.

GREENE COUNTY PUBLIC LIBRARY (XENIA)

http://www.gcpl.lib.oh.us

This site highlights a large number of community links, an online catalog, selected Internet sites, and a calendar of library events.

Harris-Elmore Public Library (Elmore)

http://library.norweld.lib.oh.us/Harris-Elmore/

A list of local history resources for researchers, plus library services, policies, and hours.

Highland County District Library (Hillsboro)

http://family.hopewell.net/hcdl/

Genealogy and local history collections are described, and there is a direct connection to OPLIN. Web reference databases include NetWellness, the huge health database housed at the University of Cincinnati, Ohio and federal government links, a dictionary and book of quotations.

Holmes County Public Library

http://www.molo.lib.oh.us/home/holmes/

More than 30% of Holmes County Library patrons are Amish, and they account for 80% of the library's circulation. This library has a pretty new building and a pretty new web page to go with it offering collection, policy and branch location information.

Hubbard Public Library

http://www.nforce.com/clients/nola/hubbard/

All the services at the Hubbard Library are detailed, along with the library's Internet policy. A list of reference databases and a link to OPLIN are also included.

HUDSON PUBLIC LIBRARY

http://clevnet.cpl.org/hudson

Membership in the Clevnet library group allows Hudson patrons to access the catalogs of more than 20 northern Ohio libraries, including the vast Cleveland Public Library. An OPLIN link appears on the first page.

HURON PUBLIC LIBRARY

http://library.norweld.lib.oh.us/Huron

A description of the library's collection is offered as well as a link to the OPLIN web page.

IDA RUPP PUBLIC LIBRARY (PORT CLINTON)

http://library.norweld.lib.oh.us/IdaRupp/
Library services, hours amd location.

KAUBISCH MEMORIAL PUBLIC LIBRARY (FOSTORIA)

http:/library.norweld.lib.oh.us/kaubisch/
Collection description, programs listing and hours.

KINSMAN FREE PUBLIC LIBRARY

http://www.kinsman.lib.oh.us/

Suggested web sites and an online Internet policy complement library services, hours and policies.

LAKEWOOD PUBLIC LIBRARY

http://www.lkwdpl.org

The Lakewood community has put together a tremendous resource for its citizens. In addition to the library's catalog, the Lakewood city home page resides here. There are pathfinders for class assignments in the local school system, sample proficiency tests to help students practice, and reference Internet resources for the global community to use.

LANE PUBLIC LIBRARY (HAMILTON)

http://purl.org/net/lanepubliclibrary/

Still under construction, this Butler County library's web page promises to include an online catalog and listing of local history resources.

LEETONIA COMMUNITY PUBLIC LIBRARY

http://www.leetonia.lib.oh.us

Library programs, Internet policy, plus a connection to OPLIN.

LEPPER PUBLIC LIBRARY (LISBON)

http://www.nforce.com/clients/nola/lepper/

Library services, Internet policies, and a link to OPLIN.

LIBERTY CENTER PUBLIC LIBRARY

http://library.norweld.lib.oh.us/LibertyCenter/

Library hours, location, services and policies.

LOGAN COUNTY DISTRICT LIBRARY (BELLEFONTAINE)

http://www.loganco.lib.oh.us

Local history resources are listed here plus a description of computer software available for public use at the library.

LORAIN PUBLIC LIBRARY

http://clevnet.cpl.org/lorain

One of many northern Ohio libraries belonging to Clevnet, Lorain's catalog accesses the holdings of all member libraries. There is a direct link to OPLIN, the electronic resource subject catalog of the Cleveland Public Library, and the opportunity for registered borrowers to check their library records and place reserves online.

LOUDONVILLE PUBLIC LIBRARY

http://www.molo.lib.oh.us/home/loudonville/

Loudonville's library catalog is online, and a group of useful search engines are linked to this page. E-mail the library, read policies and hours, or choose community links.

MACKENZIE PUBLIC LIBRARY (MADISON)

http://clevnet.cpl.org/mackenzie

One of many Clevnet libraries, Mackenzie offers an online catalog, direct link to OPLIN and the electronic resources page of the Cleveland Public Library, plus online patron information and reserves to registered borrowers.

MANSFIELD-RICHLAND COUNTY PUBLIC LIBRARY

http://www.mrcpl.lib.oh.us

This web page is as pretty as the library building, and very useful, with library policies, services, an OPLIN link, electronic resources page, and a Richland Free-Net link.

MASON PUBLIC LIBRARY

http://www2.mason-ohio.com/edsale/mason-oh/masonlibrary.html
A description of the collection and services is offered, and a direct link to NetWellness, the huge health database housed at the University of Cincinnati.

McCOMB PUBLIC LIBRARY

http://library.norweld.lib.oh.us/McComb
Local history resources, calendar of events, policies and services.

McKINLEY MEMORIAL LIBRARY (NILES)

http://www.mckinley.lib.oh.us/
Reference Internet resources including popular search engines are featured on this page, along with OPLIN, and community links.

MEDINA PUBLIC LIBRARY

http://www.medina.lib.oh.us
Medina is a CLEVNET library, which means when you search its catalog online, you're searching more than 20 other northern Ohio library catalogs as well, including the vast collection of the Cleveland Public Library. In addition to an OPLIN connection, Medina has constructed a kids page of their own, and a list of librarians' favorite sites as well as Medina county links and shortcuts to Internet search engines.

MENTOR PUBLIC LIBRARY

http://www.mentor.lib.oh.us

One of the prettiest library web pages in the state, Mentor has unique resources online like the New York Times Bestseller List, and a homework help room for kids.

MINERVA PUBLIC LIBRARY

http://www.minervaohio.com/library.htm

Download a map to the library, read about the collection and services.

MONTPELIER PUBLIC LIBRARY

http://library.norweld.lib.oh.us/Montpelier/

Description of the collection, library's policies, and a schedule of events.

MOUNT VERNON-KNOX COUNTY PUBLIC LIBRARY

http://www.knox.net/knox/library/

The most unique library web page in Ohio and definitely one of the most useful and clever, with easy access to a variety of terrific Internet sites. A set of quick links greets you at the top of the front page, linking you to such valuable sites as Ohio Lottery results, weather, and homework helpers. Yahoo is right up front and is followed with subject links to really useful Internet sites. This is as user friendly as it gets.

NELSONVILLE PUBLIC LIBRARY

http://www.seorf.ohiou.edu/~xx074/

Community links including local organizations and media are available from this library's home page, plus a link to OPLIN.

NEWCOMERSTOWN PUBLIC LIBRARY

http://www.molo.lib.oh.us/home/newcomerstown/

Community links, a map to the library, services, policies, and a selection of Internet search engines.

NEWTON FALLS PUBLIC LIBRARY

http://www.newtonfalls.lib.oh.us/

Part of the Newton Falls Information Network, this page links to government and community sites, along with OPLIN, and selected Internet sites.

NORTH BALTIMORE PUBLIC LIBRARY

http://library.norweld.lib.oh.us/North-Baltimore/

Library services and a description of the collection, plus hours and location.

OAK HARBOR PUBLIC LIBRARY

http://library.norweld.lib.oh.us/Oak-Harbor/

This site describes the many software programs available to library users on the library's computers. Other library services, policies, and hours are included.

ORRVILLE PUBLIC LIBRARY

http://www.orrville.lib.oh.us

This small library offers a huge set of resources online thanks to its participation in Clevnet. Access the catalog of Orrville and more than 20 other northeastern Ohio libraries, place a reserve online, and check your borrower record. Direct links to OPLIN, Cleveland Public Library's electronic resources page, and web search engines. Definitely the most friendly and well run library in Ohio.

PAULDING COUNTY CARNEGIE LIBRARY (PAULDING)

http://library.norweld.lib.oh.us/Paulding/

Library hours, services, location, and policies.

PEMBERVILLE PUBLIC LIBRARY

http://library.norweld.lib.oh.us/Pemberville/

Library users planning on using the Internet connection at this library might want to read the library's Internet policy posted on this web page. A list of services, collection description, and branch location and hours are included.

PERRY PUBLIC LIBRARY

http://clevnet.cpl.org/perry

As a member of Clevnet, Perry shares its catalog with more than twenty other libraries in northern Ohio. Online patrons may place reserves and check borrower records, access the electronic databases of the Cleveland Public Library and link to OPLIN.

PORTAGE COUNTY DISTRICT LIBRARY (GARRETTSVILLE)

http://www.portagecounty.lib.oh.us

This library site offers hours and locations for all system branches.

PORTER PUBLIC LIBRARY

http://ohionet.org/porter-public-library/

This is a beautiful web site full of links to community, recommended web sites, an online library catalog, event schedule, and book reviews.

PORTSMOUTH PUBLIC LIBRARY

http://ppl.library.net

Portsmouth's library catalog is online and keyword searchable, a real help to library users. Also included are library services, hours and policies.

PREBLE COUNTY DISTRICT LIBRARY (EATON)

http://www.pcdl.lib.oh.us

Geneaology information, community links plus an online library catalog.

PUTNAM COUNTY DISTRICT LIBRARY (OTTAWA)

http://www.putnamco.lib.oh.us/

Local history collection information, library services, policies, and hours.

RITTER PUBLIC LIBRARY (VERMILION)

http://clevnet.cpl.org/ritter

A member of the Clevnet library group, Ritter's online catalog simultaneously searches the catalogs of more than 20 other northern Ohio libraries. Patrons are offered access to available items from all member libraries and are able to place reserves and check their borrower records online. This site includes a direct link to OPLIN and the electronic resources page of the Cleveland Public Library.

ROCKY RIVER PUBLIC LIBRARY

http://www.rrpl.org/

Rocky River prides itself on its readers advisory, and they have brought this part of their mission to their web page. Here you will find an online version of "Between the Covers," a bimonthly book guide. Add links to OPLIN, recommended Internet sites, and the local Cowan Pottery Museum, and you have quite a useful web site.

RODMAN PUBLIC LIBRARY (ALLIANCE)

http://www.rodman.lib.oh.us/rpl/

Alliance history, genealogy links, and OPLIN. Send an e-mail question to the reference desk.

SALEM PUBLIC LIBRARY

http://www.salemohio.com/library

Library history, services, events and community links.

SANDUSKY PUBLIC LIBRARY

http://www.sandusky.lib.oh.us

Sandusky offers an online library catalog that includes the collections of more than 20 other libraries in northern Ohio belonging to the CLEVNET library consortium. OPLIN may be accessed from this page, along with local web sites for the Cleveland area.

SHAKER HEIGHTS PUBLIC LIBRARY

http://www.shpl.lib.oh.us

In addition to the vast resources found on any Clevnet library web page, Shaker has added local links that will give you a real sense of the community.

St. Marys Community Library

http://library.norweld.lib.oh.us/stmarys/
Hours, location, services and policies.

Stark County District Library

http://www.molo.lib.oh.us/home/stark/
Library services and policies, lists of new materials, and Internet links by subject.

Stow-Munroe Falls Public Library

http://www.ohionet.org/~stowpub/
Links to local schools and the Stow city home page, plus a calendar of library events.

Swanton Public Library

http://library.norweld.lib.oh.us/Swanton
Library collection description, policies, hours, and location.

Tiffin-Seneca Public Library

http://www.norweld.lib.oh.us/Tiffin-Seneca/
This pretty web page includes library hours and services, plus a list of local history resources in the library's collection.

Toledo-Lucas County Public Library

http://www.library.toledo.oh.us
This urban library has incorporated its historical photograph collection into its web page. Samples of photographs depicting Toledo's history can be viewed online with complete descriptions of each. This site also features the library's web catalog and Internet library reference resources.

Tuscarawas County Public Library (New Philadelphia)

http://www.molo.lib.oh.us/home/tuscnewphila/

The Tuscarawas library offers OPLIN training — check the online site for sign-up information. The catalog is online, and it has links to useful search engines and OPLIN.

Twinsburg Public Library

http://www.twinsburg.lib.oh.us

As a Clevnet library, Twinsburg offers a library catalog that includes holdings for over twenty northern Ohio libraries. An OPLIN connection is available from the first page and links to other Internet resources may be accessed through the electronic database section.

Upper Arlington Public Library

http://www.uapl.lib.oh.us

What a great library web site. The design of the page itself is easy to use and offers community links, maps of the area, and an extensive list of reference databases to help you answer your question online.

Warren-Trumball County Public Library

http://www.wtcpl.lib.oh.us/

This page features community links, a calendar of events, library services by department, and a link to OPLIN.

Washington-Centerville Public Library (Centerville)

http://www.wcpl.lib.oh.us

This online catalog includes a list of favorite web sites, and book lists for adults and children.

WAY PUBLIC LIBRARY (PERRYSBURG)

http://www.wcnet.org/~waylib

This site features the library's online catalog, Internet search tools, local history resources and a calendar of events.

WAYNE COUNTY PUBLIC LIBRARY (WOOSTER)

http://clevnet.cpl.org/wayne/

Another Clevnet library site with all the amenities, including a shared library catalog, links to electronic resources, search engines and branch information.

WAYNE PUBLIC LIBRARY (WAYNE)

http://library.norweld.lib.oh.us/Wayne/

Descriptions of the policies, services, and collection of the library are provided, including the local history resources so valuable to genealogists.

WESTERVILLE PUBLIC LIBRARY

http://www.wpl.lib.oh.us

Here's an example of a strong community network. Westernet is the home for Westerville schools, chamber of commerce, the city home page, visitors bureau, and Otterbein College. The library site offers an online catalog and extensive list of reference databases.

WESTON PUBLIC LIBRARY

http://library.norweld.lib.oh.us/Weston/

Branch locations, collection description, and library policies are included.

WICKLIFFE PUBLIC LIBRARY

http://www.wickliffe.lib.oh.us

The online catalog of this library accesses more than 20 other library catalogs from northern Ohio as well. A direct link to OPLIN and the electronic resources page of the Cleveland Public Library are included.

WILLIAMS COUNTY LIBRARY (BRYAN)

http://www.bryanworld.com/bpl/

History of the library, services offered by each department, plus a link to local genealogy.

WILLOUGHBY-EASTLAKE PUBLIC LIBRARY

http://www.wepl.lib.oh.us

This site starts with an Internet disclaimer, then proceeds with links to OPLIN, the Cleveland Public Library, homeschooling resources and an online reference desk.

WOOD COUNTY DISTRICT LIBRARY (BOWLING GREEN)

http://wcnet.org/WCDPL/

Bowling Green's main library offers this web page complete with online catalog, local history resources, reading lists, and online reference database links.

WORTHINGTON PUBLIC LIBRARY

http://www.worthington.lib.oh.us

Community and business links and a page for kids to call their own.

COLLEGE AND UNIVERSITY LIBRARIES

The libraries listed here are members of OhioLINK, a group of academic libraries that share resources across Ohio. Internet visitors will find links to many valuable Internet resources of a more technical and specialized nature than those found on public library catalogs. While Internet sites are available to everyone, users are not able to access subscription databases remotely unless they have arranged for these rights. If you live nearby one of these universities, it may be possible to obtain community borrowing privileges and use of these databases in house. Check with your local institution for its policy.

OhioLINK Catalog
http://www.ohiolink.edu/
Search all the OhioLINK library catalogs at once with this interface, access subject guides, Internet indexes, Ohio resources and technical reports.

BELMONT TECHNICAL COLLEGE
http://199.218.105.50/

BOWLING GREEN STATE UNIVERSITY
http://maurice.bgsu.edu/

CAPITAL UNIVERSITY
http://charli.capital.edu/

CASE WESTERN RESERVE UNIVERSITY
http://catalog.cwru.edu/

CEDARVILLE COLLEGE
http://library.cedarville.edu/

CLEVELAND STATE UNIVERSITY
http://www.ulib.csuohio.edu/

COLLEGE OF MOUNT ST. JOSEPH
http://focus.msj.edu/

CUYAHOGA COMMUNITY COLLEGE
http://innopac.tri-c.cc.oh.us/

EDISON COMMUNITY COLLEGE
http://elink.edison.cc.oh.us/

HOCKING COLLEGE
http://hockc.hocking.cc.oh.us/

KENT STATE UNIVERSITY
http://kentlink.kent.edu/

LAKELAND COMMUNITY COLLEGE
http://198.30.230.3/

MEDICAL COLLEGE OF OHIO
http://osler.mco.edu/

MIAMI UNIVERSITY
http://watson.lib.muohio.edu/

Northwest State Community College
http://nwlink.nscc.cc.oh.us

Oberlin College
http://obis.lib.oberlin.edu/

Ohio Northern University
http://polar.onu.edu/

Ohio State University
http://www.lib.ohio-state.edu/

Ohio University
http://alice.library.ohiou.edu/

Owens Community College
http://131.187.253.131/

Shawnee State University
http://library.shawnee.edu/

Southern State Community College
http://soucc.southern.cc.oh.us/

Terra Community College
http://ozz.terra.cc.oh.us/

University of Akron
http://mercury.lib.uakron.edu/

University of Cincinnati
http://ucolk2.olk.uc.edu

University of Toledo
http://utmost.cl.utoledo.edu/

WRIGHT STATE UNIVERSITY

http://wsuol2.wright.edu/

XAVIER UNIVERSITY

http://www.xu.edu/library/

YOUNGSTOWN STATE UNIVERSITY

http://jupiter.ysu.edu/

OTHER LIBRARIES

OHIOANA LIBRARY

http://www.oplin.lib.oh.us/OHIOANA

This library collects and preserves books and music by or about Ohioans. Visit its web site to search its Ohio artist database and learn more about its collections and awards.

STATE LIBRARY OF OHIO

http://winslo.ohio.gov

In addition to its online catalog, the state library provides links to state and federal government web sites, a directory of Ohio libraries, and Internet resources and search tools.

IX. The Arts

The arts are alive in Ohio, from the ballet, theatre, symphony, and open air concerts, to glorious halls of breathtaking visual arts. This chapter is devoted to the creative side of Ohio, and is loaded with virtual tour opportunities for those of us who can't be there in person. Sit back and enjoy.

Akron Art Museum
http://www.akronartmuseum.org
Current and upcoming exhibitions, an online gift shop, plus links to other museum sites.

Allen Memorial Art Museum
http://www.oberlin.edu/inside/campus_map/allen_art.html
Housed at Oberlin College, Internet visitors are able to check museum hours and view images from the collection.

Alliance of Ohio Community Arts Agencies
http://www.aok.state.oh.us/
The members of this arts groups are from all over Ohio and list their addresses, phone numbers, e-mail addresses and web pages at this site. A calendar for arts events all over Ohio is posted here, as well as links to great art sites all over the web.

AMERICAN CLASSICAL MUSIC HALL OF FAME AND MUSEUM

http://www.queencity.com/classical/

This facility located in Cincinnati held its first induction ceremony in September, 1997. Check this web site for membership information, location, facility plans, and inductee nominations.

BLOSSOM MUSIC CENTER

http://www.blossommusic.com

You have your pavilion tickets, now you want to see where you're sitting. No problem. Blossom has an online seating chart, a local map to get you there, and links to concerts all across the nation. Choose a show, link to Ticketmaster, and buy your tickets online.

BUTLER INSTITUTE OF AMERICAN ART

http://www.butlerart.com

Schedule of classes for children and adults at all sites, Butler Arts Day Camp for children, plus an online tour of the museum's collection.

CANTON ART MUSEUM

http://www.neo.lrun.com/Canton_Museum_of_Art/

Want to take some art classes? Check this site for a schedule of classes. A description of the permanent collection, traveling exhibits, and links to other art museums are also included.

CANTON BALLET

http://www.canton-ohio.com:80/cultural/ballet.html

An overview of each ballet being performed this season, plus links to the school of ballet and a portrait of the ballet's artistic director.

CANTON CIVIC OPERA

http://www.canton-ohio.com:80/cultural/opera.html

History of the group plus upcoming events.

CANTON PLAYERS GUILD

http://www.canton-ohio.com:80/cultural/guild.html

You don't have to live in New York to get good local theatre. Check this web site for a list of upcoming performances and ticket information.

CANTON SYMPHONY ORCHESTRA

http://www.canton-ohio.com:80/cultural/symphony.html

Check this season's schedule and ticket information online.

CEDAR LEE THEATRE

http://www.cedarlee.com

Information on the theatre, its performances, and an e-mail link to theatre personnel.

CINCINNATI BALLET

http://www.cincinnati.com/ballet/ballet.html

Performance and ticket information.

CINCINNATI BOYCHOIR

http://ww4.choice.net/~cbc/

Listen to this angelic choir online, order their CD's, check performance schedules, and link to other music sites.

CINCINNATI BRASS BAND

http://w3.one.net/~jwclymer/cbb.html

If you love the sound of a brass band, check out this site, listing performance schedules and links to brass band sites around the world.

CINCINNATI CHAMBER ORCHESTRA

http://w3.one.net/~cco/

Meet the orchestra, read news and reviews, get ticket information, check this season's schedule, and link to other Cincinnati area arts sites.

CINCINNATI CIVIC ORCHESTRA

http://w3.one.net/~fhunt3/cco.htm

This orchestra is the oldest all-volunteer orchestra in the U.S.. Check its web site for a schedule of performances, a short biography of the orchestra's conductor, and background on the next concert.

CINCINNATI GLORY DRUM AND BUGLE CORPS

http://ww4.choice.net/~lojik/glory/

This educational group trains youth 10-21 in competitive drum and bugle corps and brass ensemble competition. Visitors to this site may learn about the mission of the group, its program, plus view a schedule of upcoming performances.

CINCINNATI INTERNATIONAL CHORALE

http://www.iglou.com/sgrant/cic/

This talented group sings in foreign countries around the world. Check their web site for an overview of recent tours, plus concert schedules.

CINCINNATI KLEZMER PROJECT

http://members.aol.com/klezme2/index.html

This site is maintained by the students at Hebrew Union College to promote Jewish music performance. Download arrangements of Klezmer music, or a list of books vital to any Klezmer ensemble, plus link to other sites of interest.

CINCINNATILIVE ONLINE

http://www.liveinfo.com/

This interactive guide to shows and events in the Cincinnati area allows you to not only see a list of live entertainment events, but connect to area artists and clubs with web pages.

CINCINNATI MAY FESTIVAL CHORUS

http://www.iglou.com/sgrant/mayfest

This group, originally formed to celebrate the May Festival, sings with both the Cincinnati Pops and the Cincinnati Symphony. Check this web site for a history of the group, performance schedule, and links to music schools.

CINCINNATI MENS CHORUS

http://www.cincinnati.com:2001/cmchorus/

This gay male performing group offers a description of upcoming programs, reviews of recent shows, and an e-mail link to get on their mailing list or offer comments.

CINCINNATI OPERA

http://www.cincyopera.com/

Connect to this site for information on the outreach and educational programs offered by the opera, plus ticket information, history, and links to other opera sites.

CINCINNATI PERFORMING ARTS

http://w3.one.net/~jwclymer/

This is one-stop shopping for searching the performing arts in the Cincinnati area. Choose from links to orchestras, bands, jazz, chamber, vocal, dance, and theater groups plus art organization home pages.

CINCINNATI POPS ORCHESTRA

http://www.culturefinder.com/output.htm/Cincinnati_Pops_Orchestra.htm

Before you head to the Music Hall, check this web site for ticket pricing and ordering information, plus a list and description of upcoming programs.

CINCINNATI SYMPHONY ORCHESTRA

http://www.oac.ohio.gov/artstour/orchestr/cinsym.htm

Read a short history of the symphony, then check performance schedules, booking contacts, and ticket prices.

CLEVELAND AGORA

http://www.cleveland-music.com

Local music links, shows, tickets, plus history of the Agora.

CLEVELAND CENTER FOR CONTEMPORARY ART

http://www.cyberdrive.net/~ccca

Join an educational art group, e-mail for a copy of the center's newsletter, art rental and sales information, and space rental for private events.

CLEVELAND CHAMBER SYMPHONY

http://www.csuohio.edu/ccs/

Awards, schedule of performances, directions to the symphony, and portraits of symphony members.

CLEVELAND INTERNATIONAL FILM FESTIVAL

http://www.clevefilmfest.org/

Which films will be highlighted this year? Find out at this web site, plus download directions, and preview special events surrounding the festival.

CLEVELAND MUSEUM OF ART

http://www.clemusart.com

Check out upcoming Family Express or all-day drawing workshops, or search through a list of current film programs. Take a "poster tour" online, check collection highlights. Teachers: Don't miss the museum's online resource center. You'll find temporary exhibits, along with lists of classes and special events. Links to other museum web pages are provided.

CLEVELAND OPERA

http://www.clevopera.com/

Performance schedule, educational programs, ticket and seating information, plus links to other opera sites.

CLEVELAND ORCHESTRA

http://www.clevelandorch.com/

Online concert schedules, ticket information, and educational opportunities, plus a profile of the orchestra's director, a list of recordings and broadcasts by the symphony, and a look at Severance Hall.

CLEVELAND PERFORMANCE ART FESTIVAL

http://www.performance-art.org

Celebrating its 10th anniversary in 1997, this festival's web site previews events for this season's celebration.

CLEVELAND PLAYHOUSE

http://www.cleveplayhouse.org

This professional theatre company does educational outreach. Read about this service plus upcoming season performances, and history of the playhouse, then get on the playhouse mailing list via e-mail.

CLEVELAND PUBLIC THEATRE

http://www.en.com/cpt/

Get an overview of the season, submit your play for consideration, read about youth theatre education programs, and download a list of local places to visit after the performance.

CLEVELAND UNDERGROUND MUSIC ARCHIVE

http://www.worldgain.com/cuma/

An online guide to local Cleveland music including schedule and links to individual bands.

COLUMBUS MUSEUM OF ART

http://www.columbus.org/gcac/cma/index.html

In addition to collection descriptions, visitors can check a film series schedule, plus Saturday preschool workshops.

COLUMBUS OPERA

http://www.operacols.org/

Preview productions, check ticket information, special events listings, or learn about the opera's outreach programs.

COLUMBUS SYMPHONY

http://www.csobravo.org/

Performance schedules, an online ticket office, plus information about the oldest and largest arts organization in central Ohio.

CONTEMPORARY DANCE THEATER

http://www.serve.com/cdt/

Modern dance comes to life in Cincinnati, both in the theatre and classroom. This group offers its performance and class schedules at this site.

COUNCIL FOR THE ARTS OF GREATER LIMA

http://www.bright.net/~limaarts/ppframe.htm

If you're looking for a cultural experience in the Lima area, check this site for the calendar of events in your area, including art classes.

DAYTON ART INSTITUTE

http://www.amn.org/Daytext.htm

One of the largest art museums in Ohio, its web site describes the history of the institute, its location, the collection, and operating hours.

EDUCATIONAL THEATRE ASSOCIATION

http://www.etassoc.org/

This Cincinnati branch of the International Thespian Society supports educational theatre at the middle school and high school levels. If you are a drama teacher, check this page to see what ETA can do for you.

FAIRFIELD COUNTY ARTS ALLIANCE

http://www.fcaa.org/

Check this site for a schedule of current and upcoming art events and information about FCAA projects.

FINDLAY AREA ARTS COUNCIL

http://www.aok.state.oh.us/faac/

Find out what cultural events are happening in the Findlay area.

FITTON CENTER FOR THE CREATIVE ARTS

http://www.walltowall.com/fitton.htm

If you live near Hamilton, visit this online site listing current and upcoming exhibits, performances, and classes.

GREATER CINCINNATI BLUES SOCIETY

http://ourworld.compuserve.com/homepages/gcbs

Check local and regional blues events, post an advertisement for your band, or link to blues stations in the Cincinnati area.

LEBANON AREA ARTIST SERIES

http://www.fullservice.net/laas/

Purchase tickets online and check a list of upcoming events in the Lebanon area, then link to related sites.

MIAMI UNIVERSITY MUSIC DEPARTMENT

http://www.muohio.edu/

This site includes information on the Miami University Symphony, vocal ensembles, steel drum band, and opera. Audition information, music workshops, and performance schedules are included. Read a short history of the symphony, then check the performance schedule, booking contacts, and fee per performance.

MIDDLETOWN ARTS AND LECTURES SERIES

http://mumr2.mid.muohio.edu/~alseries

The Miami University campus at Middletown maintains this schedule of its lecture series, campus performing groups, and links to other noteworthy art sites.

MUSE, CINCINNATI WOMEN'S CHOIR

http://www.musechoir.org/

This group describes itself as dedicated to musical excellence and social change. Its web site offers a list of performers, a performance schedule, reviews, and information on recordings of the group available for purchase.

ODEON CONCERT CLUB

http://clever.net/realpages/odeon/

See what's playing at the Odeon.

OHIO ARTS COUNCIL

http://www.oac.ohio.gov/

Instructional program overviews, grant information, OAC publications, and a staff list are all available, plus details on the international and arts in education programs.

QUEEN CITY CHORUS

http://w3.one.net/~tmpars2/queen_city_chorus.htm

Listen to online clips of this four-part women's barbershop-harmony chorus of the Sweet Adelines International in Cincinnati, check their performance schedule, then link to any of the group's favorite web sites.

RIVERBEND MUSIC CENTER

http://www.riverbend-music.com/

Choose your favorite artist from the online schedule, then link to Ticketmaster to make the purchase. And while you're here, why not enter a Riverbend contest?

SORG OPERA COMPANY

http://www.sorgopera.com/

This performing group makes its home at the historic Sorg Opera House in Middletown. Check its web site for upcoming performances and ticket information.

SOUTHEASTERN OHIO CULTURAL ARTS CENTER

http://www.eurekanet.com/~dbarn/

Sample the current exhibit, check what's coming, or download an entry form to participate in an upcoming show.

SPRINGFIELD MUSEUM OF ART

http://spfld-museum-of-art.com

Take a virtual tour of selected art, register for museum classes via e-mail, and check the calendar of special events.

TECUMSEH OUTDOOR DRAMA

http://www.bright.net/~tecumseh/

This comprehensive site gives virtual visitors a grand tour of the Tecumseh theatre production. Written by the Ohio historian Allan Eckert, this drama is staged from June to September at the Sugarloaf Mountain Amphitheatre near Chillicothe. The web site supplies biographical information about Eckert, the music composers, artistic directors, and others involved in the drama's production. Ticket prices and reservations are available online, as are backstage tour information, policies, location, and directions.

TOLEDO MUSEUM OF ART

http://www.toledomuseum.com/

This gorgeous site gives visitors a nice preview of the great experience awaiting them at this museum. Includes museum hours and toll-free contact information.

TOLEDO OPERA

http://www.toledo-opera.com

Performance schedules and ticket information.

UNIVERSITY OF CINCINNATI BANDS

http://soa.uc.edu/

Sights and sounds, band history, plus how to join. Choose student organizations from the University's home page.

UNIVERSITY OF CINCINNATI MEN'S AND WOMEN'S CHORUS

http://uc.edu/www/

One hundred talented students from UC have placed their tour and performance schedules at this web site. Choose student organizations from the University's home page.

Verne Riffe Center for the Government and the Arts

http://www.oac.ohio.gov/riftgall/RIFFE.html

This site showcases the work of Ohio's artists and collections of the state's museums and galleries. Images of past and current exhibitions are online.

West Chester Symphony

http://w3.one.net/~jwclymer/wcm.html

This community orchestra in southwestern Ohio lists rehearsal and performance schedules on its web site.

Youngstown Symphony

http://www.neont.com/symphony.html-ssi

Upcoming events calendar, location, and contact information, including an e-mail link.

X. Consumer

Online yellow pages, relocation guides, real estate links, and better business bureaus.

AIM Relocation
http://www.suncastle.com/aim/oh.html
Ohio real estate links, moving checklist and tips, mortgage calculators, and free relocation packages for any region in Ohio.

Better Business Bureaus Serving Ohio
http://www.bbb.org/bureaus/ohio.html
Phone and fax numbers, addresses and Internet web page links to all major bureaus in Ohio. Visitors may enter a zip code to determine which bureau they should contact.

Business Resource Ohio
http://www.ohiobiz.com/busin.htm
Thousands of links to Ohio business locations and contacts arranged alphabetically.

Cleveland Ohio Real Estate
http://www.webcom.com/~greeting/welcome.html
Not just real estate listings, but a relocation salary calculator, mortgage rates, real estate newsgroups, attorneys links, and a moving checklist.

ColumbusPages

http://columbuspages.com/biz/index.html

Web site links to Columbus area businesses. Search by name or business category.

Dayton Realty Page

http://www.dayton-reality.com/

Lists what property is available in the Dayton area, complete with photos.

DreamCar.com

http://dreamcar.com/index.html

Serving the Dayton area only, car shoppers can search area promotions and specials, get a "quick quote" on a new car, or search through an online database for their "dream car."

Greater Akron Online Yellow Pages

http://www.ohio.com

Browse business categories, or enter a business name to retrieve yellow pages entries.

Homenet-Ohio

http://www.homenet.com/resident/oh/brokers.htm

If you live in one of the larger cities in Ohio, or are planning on moving to one soon, this site will give you the ability to shop for a real estate agent via your personal computer.

International Real Estate Directory-Ohio

http://www.ired.com/dir/usa/oh.htm

Links to major realty agents' web pages across Ohio.

LISTINGLINK-OHIO

http://listinglink.com/ustates/oh/

Real estate for sale in every county of Ohio — you choose amenities and price range, and this web site will match available properties.

OHIO ATTORNEY GENERAL'S OFFICE

http://www.ag.ohio.gov/

Have a complaint about bad business dealings? This site provides an online consumer complaint form.

OHIO COMMERCIAL DIRECTORY

http://www.cybernetone.com/ohio.htm

A list of Ohio businesses searchable by name or subject.

OHIO DEPARTMENT OF TAXATION

http://www.state.oh.us:80/tax/

Did you know you can download tax forms, publications, get answers to frequently asked tax questions, and look for tax statistics for the state of Ohio all on the tax department's home page? If it still doesn't make sense, this site also provides links to humans.

OHIO LOTTERY

http://www.lottotrack.com/oh/

Why wait for tomorrow's paper to check lottery results? Click on any game name from Super Lotto to Buckeye 5 for the latest lucky numbers.

OHIO REAL ESTATE
http://realestatedirectory.com/ohio.html
An online directory to realtors in a variety of Ohio cities, plus information about mortgage banking, attorneys, and insurance.

OUTLET BOUND
http://www.outletbound.com/
Type in this address for a list of Ohio outlet malls, their location, the number of stores, and a link to each of their web sites listing names of all stores inside the mall, directions, and hours.

PUBLIC UTILITIES COMMISSION OF OHIO
http://mabel.puc.ohio.gov/
This watchdog agency posts press releases on its home page to keep Ohioans abreast of the latest hearings. The complaint process is explained for those wishing to file a grievance with the commission.

REALPAGES
http://www.realpages.com
Choose a major Ohio city and link to area business yellow pages.

RELO2USA
http://www.relo2usa.com/oh-mls.htm
Select one of five Ohio cities and this site will do a real estate search and provide you with community statistics.

RENT NET

http://www.rent.net/

This site is valuable for relocating renters and buyers alike. It has great relocation-related service links including local child care, furniture rental, and moving companies. If you plan to rent, first choose from a large list of Ohio cities, select number of bedrooms and price range, and you'll be presented with a list of available units. Many units provide floor plans, photographs, and e-mail links to rental offices.

REVERSE LOOKUP

http://www.555-1212.com/whte_us.htm

Okay, so this site isn't just for Ohio, but it's so useful, who could resist? Of all the web yellow and white pages, this one features a reverse lookup, like the criss-cross directories you find at the library. Enter a phone number, say one from a classified ad, and see the name and address behind the number. Now that's useful.

TICKETMASTER

http://www.ticketmaster.com

Most tickets can be bought online now — keep this handy.

USA ONLINE-OHIO

http://www.usaol.com/OH/index.html

Online yellow pages for businesses across the entire state, from accountants to women's issues.

ZIP CODE FINDER

http://www.usps.gov/ncsc/

Zip code + 4 index for anywhere you want to send it.

XI. Employment

In addition to the huge database provided online by the Ohio Bureau of Employment Services, the State Library, Ohio EPA, Ohio State University, state government, and many private industries maintain online job listings and accept resumes via e-mail.

AkronCanton.com
http://www.akroncanton.com/
Link to area classifieds, including help wanted for the northeastern part of the state.

America's Job Bank-Ohio
http://www.ajb.dni.us/
Select for the state of Ohio, or check for openings by employer web page.

Bank One Career Navigator
http://www.bankone.com/jobs/
Surf this site for professional job openings, college training programs, and regional office addresses.

B.F. Goodrich Ohio Jobs Page

http://www.nationjob.com/bfgoodoh

This page provides a current list of job openings within the state. Click on any job title for a more detailed description, then link to the company profile to learn more about B.F. Goodrich.

Business Job Finder

http://www.cob.ohio-state.edu/~fin/jobs/jobssite.htm

Wow. What a list of internet job search pages. It may take you days, but you're sure to find the right job for you if you start here.

Career City

http://www.careercity.com/jobs/jobs.htm

Choose Ohio and your job category, and a list of jobs appears. This site also offers resume postings.

CareerPath

http://www.careerpath.com/search.html

This site takes a unique approach by collecting the classifieds from newspapers across the country. Three Ohio newspapers — the Akron Beacon Journal, Cincinnati Enquirer and Columbus Dispatch — are represented here. Make your own profile by selecting any or all of the newspapers to search, then choose a job category or keyword and the week you want to search — pretty neat.

Childrens Hospital of Columbus

http://www.childrenshospital.columbus.oh.us/

Health professionals, check the web site of this large employer, then apply online.

CINCINNATI EMPLOYMENT CLASSIFIEDS
http://careerfinder.gocinci.net/
Classifieds from the Enquirer and the Post by job category or keyword.

CLEVELAND OHIO DP CAREER CENTER
http://www.careercenter.com/oh-cleveland/index.html
If you are trained in data processing and are looking for a job, this page lists current openings in the Cleveland area plus background on the local employers who need your skills.

COLUMBUS EMPLOYMENT CONSORTIUM JOB CONNECTION
http://db.freenet.columbus.oh.us/
Advice for job searchers, information about training programs, plus online job listings.

COLUMBUS SUPERSITE- EMPLOYMENT
http://www.netwalk.com/~gccc/employ/index.html
In addition to training opportunities, this site links to major employers in the Columbus area including Nationwide Insurance, OCLC, Compuserve and the Kroger Company.

DAYTON OHIO JOBS
http://www.dayton.com/jobs.htm
Companies in the Dayton area post their job listings here. Click on the company name for one or more opening announcements.

HATTIE LARLHAM FOUNDATION

http://www.larlham.org/jobopp.html

This care provider for youth with mental retardation and developmental disabilities provided an online listing of opportunities at its main site in Mantua, four group homes, or as an independent contractor to the foundation.

HEALTH CARE EMPLOYMENT OPPORTUNITIES OHIO

http://www.hss.org/ohiojob.htm

This centralized site for health care workers lists job openings from three Ohio hospitals, then adds listings from the Ohio State Employment Office and Ohio newspapers.

MARATHON OIL EMPLOYMENT

http://www.marathon.com/recruit/index.html

Experienced professionals and college recruits can check this page for current opportunities.

NATIONAL SOCIETY OF PROFESSIONAL ENGINEERS

http://www.nspe.org/em2cloh.htm

Whether starting out or looking to move up, engineers will find a list of employment opportunities in Ohio at this organization's web site.

OHIO BUREAU OF EMPLOYMENT SERVICES

http://www.state.oh.us/obes/

Remember going to the unemployment office and using a terminal to see what job vacancies existed? Now you can access the same information from any public library or your home computer. Choose what region of the state you wish to search, and your category of work, and this database will tell you where the jobs are.

OHIO EDISON EMPLOYMENT OPPORTUNITIES

http://www.ohioedison.com/hrir.html

One of the largest employers in the state posts job ads here and accepts your resume by U.S. mail, e-mail, or fax.

OHIO EPA JOBS

http://www.epa.ohio.gov/ohr/postings.html

If the environment is your area of skill or interest, the Ohio EPA keeps a site for job listings, not only for skilled scientists, but librarians and secretarial labor as well.

OHIO HEALTH JOB OPPORTUNITIES

http://www.ohiohealth.com/jobs.htm

The OhioHealth organization spans 46 counties. Visit this site for a description of job openings and compensation packages available and links to member hospitals.

OHIO SCHOOL DISTRICT JOBS

http://www.ode.ohio.gov/www/ode/job_open.html

One-stop shopping for educators wishing to work in Ohio.

OHIO STATE HIGHWAY PATROL

http://www.odn.ohio.gov/ohp/

Trained in law enforcement? Find out if the Staties are hiring from their job opportunities link.

OHIO STATE UNIVERSITY JOB OPPORTUNITIES

gopher://gopher.acs.ohio-state.edu/11/Opportunities/

This campus is so large, it warrants its own job opportunities page, but this site lists jobs found off campus as well as on.

RILEY GUIDE

http://www.dbm.com/jobguide

Many agree that this is the single most comprehensive and useful source of job information on the web today. Although it covers the whole country, job seekers may narrow their search to Ohio and search for jobs by newsgroups for Cincinnati, Cleveland, Columbus, and the Ohio State University.

RUBBERMAID CAREERS

http://135.145.13.79/corp/careers/rj2main.htm

Facts about working for Rubbermaid, plus a list of job openings within each corporate division.

STATE OF OHIO JOB OPPORTUNITIES

http://www.state.oh.us/DAS/DHR/EMPREC.html

Want to work for the state? They have a job site all their own that includes every department and agency.

STUDENT EMPLOYMENT/ COOPERATIVE EDUCATION

http://www.westga.edu/~coop/oh.html

If you're a college student looking for work, this web site brings together several home pages of Ohio universities offering student employment and co-ops.

WORK-WEB OHIO

http://www.work-web.com/

Choose Ohio, then pick statewide or selected area listings.

YAHOO! OHIO CLASSIFIEDS

http://employment.classifieds.yahoo.com/ohio/employment/

*Browse by job category or company name or enter a city
name or job title as keyword to refine your search.*

XII. History

Ohio has much more than traditional museums. It's full of halls of fame honoring inventors, polka music, rock and roll, and pro football. And don't forget the memorials honoring Ohio's past and the ancient remnants of the moundbuilders. Each web site is gloriously visual, and contains museum exhibit information, admission prices, hours, and even "hypertours," plus thorough descriptions of each site's place in Ohio history.

ADENA

http://www.ohiohistory.org/places/adena
Home of Thomas Worthington, Ohio's sixth Governor, this restored mansion and surrounding buildings near Chillicothe are open to the public. Check the online site for a picture and description of the mansion, its history, location, admission hours and fees.

ALLEN COUNTY MUSEUM

http://www.worcnet.gen.oh.us/~acmuseum
View samples of the civil war, farm tools, minerals, locomotives, and oil collections, plus collected pictures online.

ANTI-SALOON LEAGUE HOME PAGE

http://www.wpl.lib.oh.us:80/AntiSaloon/

Housed at the Westerville Public Library, this collection documents the 40-year history of this political group. The library now offers parts of the collection via the web, including images and a classroom activity to complement your visit.

BEREA AREA HISTORICAL SOCIETY

http://members.aol.com/bereahist/index.html

Take a cybertour of the Mahler museum, check hours and location, read the online newsletter.

BUCKEYE FURNACE

http://www.ohiohistory.org/places/buckeye/

Located east of Jackson, this reconstructed blast furnace depicts a typical 19th century iron furnace operating in southeastern Ohio. Online visitors are provided with a picture of the furnace, its history, a description of the reconstructed buildings, and location information.

CAMPUS MARTIUS

http://www.ohiohistory.org/places/campus/

Site of the Northwest Territory's first organized settlement and the Ohio Company's Land Office, this museum honors Ohio's migration history. Visit the online site for history of the settlement, museum location, admission hours and fees.

CARILLON HISTORICAL PARK
http://www.classicar.com/MUSEUMS/CARILLON/CARILLON.HTM

Located in Dayton, this large park is a collection of historical buildings spread out over 65 acres representing the history of the Miami Valley. Included are a log house from 1796, a model railroad, one-room schoolhouse, print shop, Wright Hall and the Wright Flyer III. The web site gives a map of exhibits with a description and historical significance of each.

CENTERVILLE HISTORICAL SOCIETY
http://www.mvcc.net/Centerville/histsoc/

Take a walking tour, read the latest issue of the society's newsletter, and find out what's on the calendar.

CHARLIE SENS ANTIQUE AUTO MUSEUM
http://www.classicar.com/museums/sens/sens.htm

Along with a list of hours, location and admission prices, this site features links to classic car trader sites and chat rooms.

CINCINNATI CIVIL WAR ROUNDTABLE
http://members.aol.com/CintiCWRT/index.html

Book reviews, online newsletters, past presentations, and preservation efforts by a group of civil war enthusiasts in SW Ohio.

CINCINNATI HISTORICAL SOCIETY LIBRARY AND COLLECTIONS
http://www.cincymuseum.org/chscoll.htm

Link to the archives, photographs, collections, reference, and conservation departments of this historical society within a museum.

CINCINNATI MUSEUM CENTER

http://www.cincymuseum.org/index.html

Housing the Cincinnati History Museum, Museum of Natural History and Science, plus an Omnimax Theater, this site provides an online tour to both museums, the Omnimax Theater schedule, lists of school programs, as well as employment opportunities within the facility. Photographs of the original Union Terminal are online along with links to the Cincinnati Railroad Club and Amtrak. After visiting the museum, link to additional educational sites provided for educators and students.

CLEVELAND MUSEUM OF NATURAL HISTORY

http://www.cmnh.org

Read about current archaeological sites studying the Adena and Hopewell cultures of southern Ohio. Sample international visiting exhibits. Download teachers' guides on topics such as American Indians and Neighborhood Wildlife. Link to other museums around the U.S.

COLUMBUS WORLD WAR II ROUND TABLE

http://www.ohiohistory.org/ww2/index.html

This group believes strongly in oral history, and to prove it they are compiling first-person accounts of World War II from its veterans. Read these accounts, a discussion of their validity, and check upcoming meeting schedules.

CUSTER MONUMENT

http://www.ohiohistory.org/places/custer

Did you know that Custer was born in Ohio? This site marks his birthplace north of Cadiz in Harrison County. Check the online site for a short description of Custer, the bronze statue memorializing him, and monument location information.

DENNISON RAILROAD DEPOT MUSEUM

http://web1.tusco.net/rail/NewDen.html

History, schedule, and photographs of the museums' railroad collection, plus links to other sites for railroad enthusiasts.

DUNBAR HOUSE

http://www.ohiohistory.org/places/dunbar

Home of the poet Paul Laurence Dunbar, this historical museum contains many of Dunbar's original belongings. Check the online site for a short description of Dunbar's life, his significance in black American history, plus location and hours of home tours.

FAIRPORT HARBOR MARINE MUSEUM AND LIGHTHOUSE

http://www.ncweb.com/org/fhlh/

Read the history of the first Great Lakes lighthouse marine museum in the United States, see beautiful pictures of the Fairport Lighthouse, then link to other lighthouse sites in Maine.

FLINT RIDGE

http://www.ohiohistory.org/places/flint/

Located at the site of an ancient flint quarry and honoring the role of flint in the lives of prehistoric Indians, this park and museum is run by the Ohio Historical Society. Visit the web site to read about flint in Ohio's history, exhibits at the museum, plus location, hours, and admission prices.

FORT AMANDA

http://www.ohiohistory.org/places/ftamanda/

Built to protect the Northwest from British invasion, Fort Amanda is remembered with this memorial near Wapakoneta. Read about the history of the fort, and check location via this web site.

FORT ANCIENT STATE MEMORIAL

http://www.ohiohistory.org/places/ftancient/

Located southeast of Lebanon in Warren County, this archaeological site features both the Hopewell Indians and the Fort Ancient Indian civilizations. Visit the web site to learn about the earthworks found here, the museum honoring Native American tribes of Ohio, plus hiking and picnicking opportunities available in the area.

FORT HILL STATE MEMORIAL

http://www.ohiohistory.org/places/fthill/

The Hopewell Indians built an earthwork hilltop enclosure in Highland County sometime between 100 B.C. and 500 A.D. This online site describes the enclosure, its probable relation within the original village, the museum highlighting the area's archaeology and geology, plus hours and location.

FORT JEFFERSON

http://www.ohiohistory.org/places/ftjeffer/

Built to protect army supplies from the Indians, a monument and park have been constructed at the original site to commemorate this historical place. Online visitors get a good description of the role of Fort Jefferson in Ohio history, plus location and hours of the park and memorial.

FORT LAURENS

http://www.ohiohistory.org/places/ftlauren/

This museum just outside of Bolivar provides history on the Fort Laurens campaign and the fort's construction, displays artifacts unearthed at the site, and includes the tomb of Ohio's unknown patriot, honoring the heroes of the American Revolutionary War. Its online site provides a brief history of the fort, directions to the site, plus admission hours and fees.

FORT MEIGS

http://www.ohiohistory.org/places/ftmeigs/

Built by William Henry Harrison in 1813 to protect the area from British invasion, this reconstruction of the fort plus other surrounding buildings lies in Perrysburg, Ohio. Its online site provides visitors with a description of the grounds, its history, plus directions to the site, hours and admission costs.

FORT RECOVERY STATE MEMORIAL

http://www.ohiohistory.org/places/ftrecovr/

Originally built at the site of General Arthur Sinclair's defeat at the hands of the Miami Indians, Fort Recovery has been reconstructed along with a stockade and museum. Visit the online site provided by the Ohio Historical Society to learn about the fort's history, the memorial's location, hours, and admission costs.

GLACIAL GROOVES

http://www.ohiohistory.org/places/glacial/

Eighteen thousand years ago, a glacier moved through northern Ohio and left grooves in the limestone bedrock that are still visible today. This fossilized area on Kelly's Island is described online, complete with a picture of the grooves, a history of its formation, and viewing location.

GLENDOWER

http://www.ohiohistory.org/places/glendowe/

Home of John Milton Williams, a framer of the state's constitution, this site's page contains a description and history of the mansion, plus location, hours, and admission fees.

GRANT BIRTHPLACE

http://www.ohiohistory.org/places/grantbir/

Near the mouth of Indian Creek at the Ohio River lies this small cottage where the famous civil war general and U.S. President was born. Visit this site to read the history of the building, its location, hours, and fees for admission.

GRANT SCHOOLHOUSE

http://www.ohiohistory.org/places/grantschl

The Ohio Historical Society has preserved the small schoolhouse in Georgetown, Ohio, where Ulysses Grant attended classes, and has provided a web page describing Grant, his teachers, and the history surrounding the building. In addition, this site lists location, hours, and admission fees.

HANBY HOUSE

http://www.ohiohistory.org/places/hanby/

The home of the composer of "Darling Nelly Gray" has a web site listing hours, location, admission price, plus a short description of the house and its contents.

HARDING HOME

http://www.ohiohistory.org/places/harding/

The site of President Warren Harding's wedding, and his residence for 30 years before his election to the Presidency, this was the place where Harding conducted his famous "front porch campaign." Learn about the house, Harding's careers before his Presidency, plus hours, location, and admission fees to this historical site.

HARDING TOMB

http://www.ohiohistory.org/places/hardtomb/

One of many presidential memorials in Ohio, this tomb's web site lists location, hours, plus a short description of the site's architecture.

HARRISON TOMB

http://www.ohiohistory.org/places/harrison/

Read about our ninth president's career, the monument in his honor, its location, and hours available to the public.

HAYES PRESIDENTIAL CENTER

http://www.rbhayes.org/

Rutherford B. Hayes, one of many presidents from Ohio, is enshrined here, complete with residence, library and museum. Visit this site for information on the history preserved here, plus hours, location, and admission fees.

HEISEY GLASS

http://www.infinet.com/~lstevens/heisey/

Antique glass collectors are very familiar with this Newark company which manufactured glassware from 1896 to 1957. At this web site collectors can read company history, see examples of Heisey glassware, view old company magazine advertisements, and link to the Heisey Collectors of America's web site.

INDIAN MILL

http://www.ohiohistory.org/places/indian/

A restored mill along the Sandusky River, Indian Mill's web site offers location, hours, admission price, and a good description of the mill's history.

INSCRIPTION ROCK

http://www.ohiohistory.org/places/inscript/

Another site of ancient pictographs dating between 1200 and 1600 AD, the web site offers historical information, location, accessibility, hours, and admission fees.

INTERNATIONAL WOMEN'S AIR AND SPACE MUSEUM

http://www.infinet.com/~iwasm

This site features biographies of women aviation pioneers, including NASA astronaut biographies with photographs of each subject.

INVENTURE PLACE

http://www.invent.org

The National Inventors Hall of Fame is much more than a collection of exhibits honoring famous inventors. Inventure place is designed to be a "laboratory where you can explore your curiosity and creativity." Selected exhibits complete with audioclips are available at this web site, along with an online index of inventions and inventor biographies, ideal for home reference.

LAKE ERIE ISLANDS HISTORICAL SOCIETY

http://www.leihs.org

Learn what this active society has planned for the upcoming season, including lectures, tours, and programs for children. Link to a site for history on the Battle of Lake Erie.

LARRY STEVENS WEB SITE

http://www.infinet.com/~lstevens/

Calling all Civil War buffs. Mr. Stevens has put together some great links for you to enjoy, including "Ohio in the Civil War," a variety of infantry sites, letters, and civil war booksellers.

LEO PETROGLYPH

http://www.ohiohistory.org/places/leopetro/

Petroglyphs are prehistoric Indian inscriptions — something you'd probably associate with the southwestern United States. Ohio has several of these remains, carved in sandstone and available for public viewing. This site gives you location and directions, historical significance, plus information on hours and admission fees.

LOGAN ELM

http://www.ohiohistory.org/places/loganelm/

Answering a favorite question of Ohio schoolchildren, this historically significant tree died in 1965. Marked by a plaque and surrounded by monuments honoring Native Americans, this park is located near Circleville. Visit the online site to learn the historical significance of the old elm tree, plus location information.

LYME VILLAGE

http://www.onebellevue.com/lymevillage/index.html

This collection of historical buildings in Bellevue may be viewed online, and visitors are provided with a nice history of the preservation of the area. A calendar of events is provided, plus contacts for further information.

McKINLEY MUSEUM AND NATIONAL MEMORIAL

http://www.neo.lrun.com/McKinley_Museum/index.html

View the historical artifacts of William McKinley, prehistoric artifacts from Nobles Pond, then travel through the street of shops to see what life was like at the turn of the century. Check classes and summer camp offerings at the museum's Discover World and planetarium online.

MIAMISBURG MOUND

http://www.ohiohistory.org/places/miamisbg/

Contructed by the ancient Adena Indians, this is the largest conical burial mound in Ohio. Visit the online site for a description of the mound, visitors' area, and location information.

MOUNDBUILDERS STATE MEMORIAL

http://www.ohiohistory.org/places/moundbld/

Preserved geometric earthworks and a museum exhibiting prehistoric Ohio artwork are the focal points of this state memorial. Visit the online site to learn about the site's significance in Hopewell culture, its size, construction, location, and hours of admission.

MUSEUM OF CERAMICS

http://www.ohiohistory.org/places/ceramics/

Honoring the ceramics produced in the East Liverpool area, this museum includes exhibits on pottery production methods and East Liverpool history. Visit this online site for a description of the museum, its holdings, plus location, hours, and admission fees.

NATIONAL AFRO-AMERICAN MUSEUM AND CULTURAL CENTER

http://www.ohiohistory.org/places/afroam/

Located on the campus of Wilberforce University, this museum's exhibits honor all eras of African-American culture and history. Visit the online site to read about the museum's collections, location, hours, and admission fees.

NATIONAL CLEVELAND-STYLE POLKA HALL OF FAME

http://www.clevelandstyle.com/polkahall

Created by the American-Slovenian Polka Foundation, this site lists greatest all-time songs and annual achievement awards.

NATIONAL ROAD/ZANE GRAY MUSEUM

http://www.ohiohistory.org/places/octagon/

This museum serves three functions — first, to memorialize the great National Road that linked the early American frontier to the eastern coast, second, to honor Zanesville author Zane Gray, master of the western genre, and third, to depict the history of Ohio art pottery. Online visitors are provided with a description of the museum's exhibits, a picture of the museum, a short history of the National Road, plus information on location, hours, and admission fees.

NEIL ARMSTRONG AIR AND SPACE MUSEUM

http://www.3d-interact.com/SpaceMuseum

Following a brief history of Neil Armstrong's role in space exploration, this site offers lunar links, including image browsers that provide gorgeous photos of our moon.

OBERLIN HISTORY

http://ocaxp1.cc.oberlin.edu/~EOG/

The Electronic Oberlin Group has put together quite an impressive project documenting the history of the area, including biographies of influential people, histories of organizations, images of historic landmarks, and historical records.

OCTAGON EARTHWORKS

http://www.oplin.lib.oh.us/OHS2/site/sites/central/octag.html
Built by the Hopewell Indians near Newark, Ohio, these mounds were probably used for religious purposes. Visit the online site for a description and history of the site, plus location and hours.

OHIO CERAMIC CENTER

http://www.ohiohistory.org/places/ohceram/
Zanesville, Roseville, and Crooksville pottery are honored at this museum in Perry County. Visit the online site for a description of the museum's exhibits, a history of pottery in this area, plus location, hours, and admission fees.

OHIO CIVIL WAR STORIES

http://www.infinet.com/~lstevens/a/stori/
Civil War enthusiasts — bookmark this page. Dozens of links to letters and tales of Ohio Civil War units are listed on this page, sure to bring hours of reading pleasure.

OHIO HISTORICAL RECORDS ADVISORY BOARD

http://www.ohiohistory.org/ohrab/index.html
Read what this planning board has decided about the future of Ohio historical records and their electronic conversion.

OHIO HISTORICAL SOCIETY

http://www.ohiohistory.org/

This nonprofit society exists to "promote a knowledge of archeology and history, especially in Ohio." If you've ever visited the Ohio Historical Center north of Columbus, or the many sites around the state maintained by the society, you know OHS leads the way in preservation for our state. Visit this beautiful web site to learn more about OHS's preservation efforts, read a calendar of events, and travel back through time on the Time Travelers Kids Page.

OHIO NETWORK OF AMERICAN HISTORY RESEARCH CENTERS

http://www.ohiohistory.org/lgr/networkl.html

This site links to the eight centers across the state located mainly in universities which are under the jurisdiction of the state archives and qualify as research centers for American History.

OHIO NEWSPAPER INDEXES

http://winslo.ohio.gov/ohnewsindex.html

If you're looking for an obituary or an event within the last 20 years, try these online indexes to several Ohio newspapers.

OHIO RIVER MUSEUM

http://www.ohiohistory.org/places/ohriver/

Located in downtown Marietta, this museum houses three exhibits depicting the river's natural history, the steamboat age, and man's enduring relationship with the river. Floating on the Muskingum River just outside the museum is the W.P. Snyder Jr., a remnant of the steam-powered era. Visit this online site for a description of the museum, plus location, admission hours and fees.

OHIO STATEHOUSE

http://www.ohiohistory.org/places/statehse/

One of the oldest state houses in the country, this recently restored center of Ohio government is open to the public. Online visitors are provided with a picture of the building, a discussion of its history and architecture, plus a tour schedule and location information.

OHIO VILLAGE

http://www.ohiohistory.org/places/ohvillag/

History comes alive at this large recreation of a Civil War era town. Spread out over 58 acres adjacent to the Ohio Historical Center north of downtown Columbus, programs and exhibits change seasonally and tours are given by costumed guides. For a schedule of current and future programs, hours, and admission fees, check this online site.

OHIO'S HISTORIC CANALS

http://www.infinet.com/~lstevens/canal/

The preservation of Ohio's Canal areas has been a hot topic lately, with lots of hiking and biking trails being built along the old waterways. In addition to a short history of the canal system in Ohio and a canal map, this site tells visitors what remains where and what recreational opportunities are available.

OUR HOUSE

http://www.ohiohistory.org/places/ourhouse/

This three-story tavern built in 1819 has been restored in Gallipolis. Visit online for a picture of the tavern, its history, plus location, hours, and admission fees.

PIQUA HISTORICAL AREA

http://www.ohiohistory.org/places/piqua/

The farm of John Johnston, an Indian agent for western Ohio from 1812 to 1830, is the highlight of this preserve in northwestern Ohio. Read about the history of the farm, the restored section of the Miami and Erie Canal that runs through the site, the reconstructed canalboat of W.H. Harrison, plus check location and hours for the area.

PORTAGE COUNTY HISTORICAL SOCIETY

http://www2.clearlight.com/~pchs/

Short stories about Portage County history are the highlight of this page which also includes a photo gallery, genealogy, and links to search engines.

PRO FOOTBALL HALL OF FAME

http://www.canton-ohio.com/hof

If you love football, you'll find lots to like here. Team histories, biographies of all enshrinees, plus a small virtual tour of the hall are included. Weekly statistics are updated throughout the regular NFL season, then archived in "Football Decade by Decade."

RANKIN HOUSE

http://www.ohiohistory.org/places/rankin/

Staunch abolitionist and conductor on the underground railroad, the home of this Presbyterian minister has been restored for guided tours. Learn about John Rankin's antislavery activities, his house, and the steps to freedom extending from the Ripley streets below to the Rankin house on top of Lookout Hill. Location, hours, and admission fees are also listed at this site.

ROCK AND ROLL HALL OF FAME

http://www.rockhall.com

This site is multimedia city. Listen to inductees speeches, tour virtual exhibits, enter contests online, and experience virtual reality with online QuickTime videos.

SAUDER VILLAGE

http://www.a1.com/sauder/

Skilled craftsmen and costumed interpreters are part of what you'll see at the web site for this living history complex in northwest Ohio. In addition to highlights of the village, there is a calendar of events, and directions to nearby lodging and restaurants.

SCHOENBRUNN VILLAGE

http://www.ohiohistory.org/places/schoenbr/

Founded in 1772 as a mission to the Delaware Indians by the Moravian Church and abandoned during the Revolutionary War, the Ohio Historical Society has reconstructed this village and original cemetery. Read about the Moravians, their legacy, the museum and village, plus check location, hours, and admission fees.

SEIP MOUND

http://www.ohiohistory.org/places/seip/

Built by the Hopewell Indians for burial purposes, this mound near Chillicothe is open to the public. Check the online site for a description of the site, its history, location, and hours.

SERPENT MOUND

http://www.ohiohistory.org/places/serpent

Located in Adams county, this is the largest serpent effigy in the United States. Its online site describes the significance of the mound, the museum nearby, plus location, admission hours and fees.

SHAKER HISTORICAL MUSEUM

http://www.ohiohistory.org/places/shaker/

Celebrating the legacy of simplicity, equality, freedom and justice, this site describes the collection of surviving Shaker objects, most of which remain from the North Union colony in what is now the city of Shaker Heights. Location, hours, and admission fees are included.

STATEHOUSE HISTORY

http://www.statehouse.state.oh.us/ahist.html

The Ohio Statehouse in Columbus is one of the oldest statehouses in the U.S. still in use. This online guided tour will take you through the glories of yesterday and the preservation recently completed on this magnificent building.

STOWE HOUSE

http://www.ohiohistory.org/places/stowe/

Often described as the woman who started the civil war, Harriet Beecher Stowe lived in this Cincinnati house from 1833 to 1850. Now a cultural and educational center, online visitors are provided with a picture of the house, a short history of it and Stowe's work, plus location, hours, and price of admission.

SUMMIT COUNTY HISTORICAL SOCIETY

http://www.neo.lrun.com/Summit_County_Historical_Society

This lovely site lets you tour the museum while describing the exhibits and collection.

UNITED STATES AIR FORCE MUSEUM

http://www.wpafb.af.mil/museum

This site is huge. Online visitors can spend hours taking virtual tours and combing through aircraft history, weapon and engine galleries, and if you still haven't had your fill, there are plenty of related sites listed.

USS COD HOME PORT

http://www.en.com/users/usscod/

Take a virtual tour, check hours of operation, or read articles about this World War II submarine on display in Lake Erie. Includes links to other maritime museums and photos.

YOUNGSTOWN HISTORICAL CENTER OF INDUSTRY AND LABOR

http://www.ohiohistory.org/places/youngst

Chronicling the rise and fall of the Mahoning Valley steel industry, this museum's site includes a nice description of the museum's displays, plus location, hours, and admission fee information.

ZOAR VILLAGE

http://www.ohiohistory.org/places/zoar

In the early 19th century, German settlers who had separated from the Lutheran church began a commune at Zoar. Today the village is restored and visitors are given guided tours into the world of this historical settlement. Before you pack the car, take a virtual tour of the bakery, store, tinsmith shop, blacksmith shop, and greenhouse, check hours and tour fees, then take a ride to see it for yourself.

XIII. Genealogy

Genealogy depends on historical records, and Ohio has converted a vast amount to electronic format. Along with the Ohio Online Death Certificate Index, cybersurfers from across the country can also locate the census records, birth, marriage or cemetery records that are vital to their family research by searching public library catalogs online. Many genealogical societies have home pages with e-mail links for queries from anywhere around the world. Listed below are sites loaded with Ohio genealogy information.

ATHENS COUNTY GENEALOGICAL CHAPTER
http://www.seorf.ohiou.edu/~xx024/
This gorgeous site is loaded with links for family researchers, including Athens County records, pioneer, civil war and Afro-American family records, and links to huge genealogy databases around the country.

DARKE COUNTY OHIO GENEALOGICAL RESEARCHERS HOME PAGE
http://php.ucs.indiana.edu/~jetorres/dco.html
Early census indexes (1820-50), section maps, history of towns and townships, plus links to nearby Indiana sites. Link from here to the Darke County Genealogy fair, where you may submit a query, check county marriage records from 1817-1850, and lists of civil war veterans.

DELAWARE COUNTY GENEALOGY

http://www.owu.edu/~grcryder/index.html

It's always helpful when a site provides tips for doing genealogy in its area, and this site does that and so much more. There is a map to help you get to the Delaware Historical Society, an online library catalog, links to research materials and information about research services.

EVERTON'S GENEALOGICAL HELPER

http://www.everton.com/usa/oh.htm

Addresses of Family History Centers in Ohio, research outlines for Ohio, county outline maps, plus lots of advice on research methods.

MARION COUNTY HISTORICAL AND GENEALOGICAL SOCIETIES

http://genealogy.org/~smoore/marion.html

If your ancestors are from Marion County, you're in luck. This site tells you which records are available and links you to other people doing research in the area. Searchable databases at this site include records from the penitentiary, infirmary, and mortality census.

MIAMI COUNTY GENEALOGICAL RESEARCHERS HOMEPAGE

http://members.aol.com/cporcher/miamico/miacoindex.html

This site is loaded with links to census records, place names, section maps, and histories for the area. There's a list of local researchers for those visitors looking for contacts.

MIAMI VALLEY GENEALOGICAL INDEX
http://www.pcdl.lib.oh.us/miami/miami.htm

Type in a surname and this index searches marriage, tax, and census records for Darke, Greene, Hamilton, Mercer, Miami, Montgomery, Preble, Shelby, Warren, Butler and Champagne counties.

OHIO GENEALOGICAL SOCIETY
http://www.ogs.org/public/default.htm

This large organization collects and publishes many resources, including Bible records, family and county histories, all Ohio censuses, and atlases. Visit this online site to search the society's research library, chapter addresses and links, or post a query on the online bulletin board.

OHIO HISTORICAL SOCIETY GENEALOGICAL SOURCES
http://winslo.ohio.gov/ohswww/gensourc.html

This online guide tells researchers which birth, death, census, land entry, marriage and naturalization records are housed at the society, what records exist statewide, and how to access them. Included is the Ohio Online Death Certificate Index, which, upon completion, will index Ohio death records from 1908-1944.

OHIO NEWSPAPER INDEXES ONLINE
http://winslo.ohio.gov/ohnewsindex.html

If you're looking for an obituary or an event within the last 20 years, try these online indexes to several Ohio newspapers. Links to Akron Beacon Journal, Cleveland Plain Dealer, Cleveland Magazine, Ohio Magazine, Dayton Daily News, Northern Ohio Live, and Cleveland Press indexes, plus obituaries from the 1970's and 1980's.

OHIO ONLINE DEATH CERTIFICATE INDEX

http://www.on-library.com/cgi-onlib/ohiohist/dindex.pl

A searchable index covering 1913-1917 deaths in Ohio, eventually covering 1908-1944. For information about how to obtain records for other years, choose a link from this site.

OHIO RECORDS ON THE US GENWEB PROJECT

http://www.netwalk.com/~coliver/ohio/records.htm

This site holds a tremendous amount of information, including a chart showing earliest available birth, marriage, death, land, probate, and court records for each Ohio county.

OMII GENEALOGY PROJECT AND KIDRON HERITAGE CENTER

http://www.bright.net/~swisstea/

Search information on Swiss Mennonite and German Amish ancestors, e-mail a query, submit your family information, and link to related databases.

ROOTSWEB-OHIO RESOURCES

http://www.rootsweb.com/roots-l/USA/oh.html

This site is the Ohio portion of the huge group of ROOTS-L files that make up this comprehensive database. Search by surname, find out what books on Ohio genealogy the Library of Congress owns, download a list of Ohio genealogical societies, and find out where to write for Ohio vital records. Definitely one of the most comprehensive sites, this should be a first stop for all Ohio family researchers. Ohio county genealogical project pages appear as links at this site, making it a potential first stop for all Ohio family researchers.

SHELBY COUNTY GENEALOGY
http://www.dallas.net/~rwiley/shelby/shelby.htm
An online guide to the history, cemeteries, and local records of Shelby County. Includes a link for queries.

STARK COUNTY OHIO GENEALOGICAL RESEARCHERS HOME PAGE
http://www.webcom.com/schori/stark.html
Guide to Stark County resources including vital records, obituaries, early settlers, and surname indexes.

TOLEDO AREA GENEALOGICAL SOCIETY
http://www.utoledo.edu/homepages/drostet/tags/index.htm
Besides membership info and meeting dates, there is an e-mail form for queries should your ancestors hail from Lucas County.

XIV. Environment

If you think the Environmental Protection Agency is alone in the fight to keep Ohio's natural resources healthy, spend some time with these sites. Read the latest studies, assessments, and state of the environment reports from groups across the Buckeye State, and learn the science behind the beauty around us.

CLERMONT COUNTY ENVIRONMENTAL RESOURCES DIRECTORY

http://www.clc.uc.edu/~marcotfa/environ/envredir.htm

If you're a Clermont County resident, you've been provided with a wealth of online links to county and state water quality, hazardous materials, and air quality links. Includes hotlines for emergency spill response, gas problems, and poison control. The state links are of great value to any Ohio resident.

EARTH DAY COALITION

http://bbs2.rmrc.net/~earthday

Northeast Ohio is the home for this non-profit environmental education group. Visit the home page to find out about programming, training, internships, and publishing activities.

GREAT LAKES BIODIVERSITY

http://epawww.ciesin.org/glreis/nonpo/onlin_res/TNC/glbio.html

Developed at the Nature Conservancy's Great Lakes Program Office, this site provides information on the Great Lakes basin for laymen. Track nature heritage programs, conservation efforts, and wetlands inventory data.

GREAT LAKES ENVIRONMENTAL DIRECTORY

http://eelink.umich.edu/GLED.html

Search this regional directory by organization name, city, state, organization type, activities, or keywords.

GREAT LAKES FORECASTING SYSTEM HOMEPAGE

http://superior.eng.ohio-state.edu/

Ohio State University's Department of Civil and Environmental Engineering and Geodetic Science maintains this site, showing forecast and "nowcast" images, research, and related www servers.

GREAT LAKES INFORMATION NETWORK

http://www.great-lakes.net/

Lake Erie facts, areas of concern, plus links to Lake Erie water temperature maps (updated every six hours), lake management plans, and spatial data viewers.

GREAT LAKES PROTECTION FUND

http://epawww.ciesin.org/glreis/nonpo/norg/gl_prot_fund/Protection-fund.html

Created by the governors of the Great Lakes states and established in 1989, this organzation awards grants to prevent toxic pollution and remove its effects from the lakes and their watersheds. This site includes the goals, mission, and strategies identified by the fund, plus information on applying for grants.

GREAT LAKES REGIONAL ENVIRONMENTAL INFORMATION SYSTEM

http://epawww.ciesin.org/

This is a comprehensive environmental site for the northern region, with links to environmental databases, descriptions of regional initiatives, and an overview of state level programs. Includes an extensive bibliography and links to regional environmental organizations, plus detailed recovery plans for major rivers in the Lake Erie watershed.

LAKE ERIE HOME PAGE

http://sparky.nce.usace.army.mil/erie.html

Forecasted and recorded data for Lake Erie, including lake levels and storm probability tables.

LAKE ERIE LAKEWIDE MANAGEMENT PLAN

http://chagrin.epa.ohio.gov/lamp/index.html

Supported by the Ohio Environmental Protection Agency, this page includes a concept paper, glossary of terms, and updated fact sheets. A link gives citizens ideas on how they can be involved in the management of Ohio's great lake.

NATIONAL WEATHER SERVICE LAKE ERIE MARINE INFORMATION

http://www.csuohio.edu/nws/marine/marine.html

Before you venture out on the lake for a day of boating pleasure, visit this site for open waters forecasts, marine warnings and statements, current wave heights and directions, and lake surface temperatures.

N.E. OHIO ENVIRONMENTAL DATA EXCHANGE NETWORK(NEO-EDEN)

http://cua6.csuohio.edu/~ucweb/neoeden/neoeden.htm

Universities across Ohio collect and analyze environmental data, then post their findings at this web site.

OHIO ENVIRONMENTAL COUNCIL

http://www.greenlink.org/oec/index.html

OEC supplies environmental technical assistance and education, lobbies and monitors state government. Find out about this 120-member conservation organization and its activities from their home page.

OHIO FUND FOR THE ENVIRONMENT

http://bbs2.rmrc.net/~earthday/ohiofund.html

Find out about this benevolent fund for environmental and conservation organizations.

OHIO RIVER INFORMATION

http://www.orsanco.org/index.html

Quick facts, navigation information, and environmental statements on the river.

OHIO RIVER ORGANIZATIONS

http://www.irn.org/rivorg/rivorgoh.html

Here's who's working to save and strengthen Ohio's rivers.

OHIO WEATHER FORECASTS

http://iwin.nws.noaa.gov/iwin/oh/state.html

State forecasts and up-to-date conditions from the National Weather Service.

RECYCLING

http://www.dnr.state.oh.us/odnr/recycling/recycling.html

What's the newest recycling technology? Who's doing their share in Ohio? What grants are available to communities through the Recycle Ohio Grant program? Find out here.

SIERRA CLUB OHIO CHAPTER

http://www.greenlink.org/sierra/

Keep up to date on what's happening with Ohio environmental legislation. Read about local Sierra Club community campaigns, check outing calendars. Includes links to environmental sites nationwide.

STATE OF THE ENVIRONMENT REPORT

http://www.epa.ohio.gov/other/comprsk/new/ff.html

Ohio's air quality, drinking water, natural resource use, and environmental risk are analyzed in this online report from the Ohio Environmental Protection Agency.

U.S. GEOLOGICAL SURVEY PROGRAMS IN OHIO

http://h2o.usgs.gov/public/wid/html/oh.html

For those interested in the science behind Ohio's natural beauty, this site links to flood and drought studies, shoreline erosion on Lake Erie, water-quality assessments and investigations, coal studies, and landslide hazards within the state.

WATER QUALITY LABORATORY OF HEIDELBERG COLLEGE

http://www.heidelberg.edu/WQL

Information on private well testing programs, publications, and data sets.

XV. HEALTH

Ohio has a set of health resources all its own. Cincinnati hospitals offer online health encyclopedias and indexes via the state funded online health network NetWellness. This huge database also contains directories to health professionals and agencies in Ohio. "Ohio-Link" and community web pages offer links to local hospitals and physicians. The nationally recognized medical schools at Ohio's leading universities offer pages of links to a myriad of medical subjects covering every aspect of advanced health care. Try these links and take a trip through the world of Ohio medicine.

AIDS TASK FORCE OF GREATER CLEVELAND

http://www.atfgc.org/

This URL takes you to Lifelines, the online newsletter of the ATFGC. In it you'll find information on programs available to AIDS victims, including bus fare to medical appointments and financial aid programs. Articles discuss issues close to home for aids sufferers and caregivers. Included are links to other aids-related sites across the country.

CLEVELAND CLINIC FOUNDATION

http://www.ccf.org/CCFMain.html

Request an appointment online, search the patient care information section, or get an overview of the research institute's activities. For health professionals, there is a link to educational opportunities at the clinic, including nursing, graduate, and continuing medical education.

CLEVELAND HEALTH MUSEUM

http://healthmuseum.org/

The primary objective of this museum is to educate and visitors to the online site can browse through a long list of programming events for both youth and adults. Current exhibits are described at this site as well as links to museum staff and information on renting the museum for your group.

DENTAL GLOBE

http://dentalglobe.com/doh.html

Click on an Ohio city and receive a list of dentists practicing in that area.

HEALTH ALLIANCE OF GREATER CINCINNATI

http://www.health-alliance.com/

These health topics provided by Cincinnati hospitals offer sound advice on women's health, occupational health, oncology, sports medicine, cardiac care and more.

HEALTH WEB

http://bones.med.ohio-state.edu/hw/ref/

Maintained by the Prior Health Sciences Library at the Ohio State University, this site features health associations, dictionaries, directories, research, statistics and health news. An online ready reference collection is available, including The Merck Manual and an online version of International Classification of Diseases.

MEDICAL COLLEGE OF OHIO

http://www.mco.edu:80/sites/medsites.html

The section "Useful Health-Related Websites" is a gold mine for online health information. Topics include neuroscience, anatomy, physiology, telemedicine, alternative medicine and dermatology, as well as links to medical organizations.

MT. SINAI MEDICAL LIBRARY

http://www.mtsinai.org/leftlist.html

Quick reference, subject links, plus information on maternity and nutrition issues.

NetWellness

http://ovchin.uc.edu/

What a great way to spend taxpayers' money. NetWellness defines itself as an "electronic consumer health library." Although the world wide web database is huge, visitors accessing NetWellness from dedicated sites across Ohio and neighboring states also have access to the Physician's Desk Reference, Merck Manual, Medline, and the Personal Medical Advisor. Ask your local library or university if they have this special link. Either way, this is a one-stop site for laymen. "Hot Topics" provides links to the most sought after medical information, such as nutrition, stroke, diabetes, and health care plans. "Ask an Expert" starts with a disclaimer reminding you that online information is not meant to take the place of a medical professional. You must agree to this disclaimer before proceeding to topics such as breast cancer, pregnancy, smoking, children's health, and infant care. "In the News" links to both CNN Interactive and USA Today Health for the latest media stories on medical topics.

Northeastern Ohio Universities College of Medicine

http://www.neoucom.edu/

In addition to department home pages, this medical college's site has links to "off-site resources" including the Harvard BioPages, the American Medical Association home page, and biomedical sites.

Ohio Area Agencies on Aging

http://www.aoa.dhhs.gov/aoa/webres/area-oh.htm

This site provides nice links for seniors on health plus links to local agencies which can provide more information.

OHIO DEPARTMENT OF HEALTH
http://www.state.oh.us/doh/
Health statistics, recent press releases, state health regulations and rules, pending rules and hearings, plus links to other health-related sites.

OHIO DEPARTMENT OF MENTAL HEALTH
http://www.mh.state.oh.us/
This government site offers links to community mental health information, news and announcements, reference materials, plus an e-mail link for specific questions or comments.

OHIO DEPARTMENT OF MENTAL RETARDATION AND DEVELOPMENTAL DISABILITIES
http://www.state.oh.us/dmr
Contact information and mission statement for this government agency are featured.

OHIO NORTHERN UNIVERSITY COLLEGE OF PHARMACY
http://www.onu.edu/Pharmacy/
Click on "Pharmacy Links on the Internet" for a selection of drug and health-related web sites. "Virtual Hospital" is especially useful if you choose the health care provider information. Here you will find discussion of various body systems, their health, diseases, and common procedures performed on them. There is also a multimedia textbook link on the ONU site for those interested in furthering their medical knowledge.

OHIO PHARMACISTS ASSOCIATION
http://www.ohiopharmacists.org

Even if you're not a member, you'll find the pharmacy-related web sites available here of great value, such as the American Cancer Society's home page, "managing your Diabetes," Alzheimer's Association, the Merck Manual, and a trial subscription to Mosby's Complete Drug Reference.

OHIO PODIATRIC MEDICAL ASSOCIATION
http://www.opma.org/

This site's "virtual medical marketplace" links to major healthcare corporations' web pages. The continuing medical education section links to award winning medical sites in addition to a large number of podiatry-related and general medical web pages. There is a members' fax and e-mail list.

OHIO STATE UNIVERSITY CANCER CENTER
http://www-cancer.med.ohio-state.edu/osuccc.htm

Information on cancer prevention and treatment, including basic research, clinical trials, and oncology.

OHIO STATE UNIVERSITY COLLEGE OF PHARMACY
http://www.pharmacy.ohio-state.edu/

The pharmacy-related links found on this page are for both the professional and the layman. Of particular use is the "Pharmaceutical Information Network" with links to drug FAQ's, and a "disease center" which provides information on research and treatment for many major diseases including those affecting the cardiovascular, digestive, neurological and respiratory systems.

RAINBOW BABIES AND CHILDRENS HOSPITAL
http://users.multiverse.com/~mlsalin/rainbow.html
Parents will find the pediatric links found here of special interest.

ST. LUKE'S MEDICAL CENTER
http://www.en.com/stlukes/
Advice on finding a doctor, plus links to the medical library.

STATE BOARD OF NURSING
http://www.state.oh.us/nur/
Nursing law and online verification of licensure.

STATE INJURY MORTALITY STATISTICS
http://www.cdc.gov/ncipc/osp/states/3901.htm
From the Centers for Disease Control, these Ohio statistics include Ohio death rates by age and sex for several years.

STATE MEDICAL BOARD
http://www.state.oh.us/med/
Have questions about specialists or malpractice histories? This site tells you the Board's purpose and provides an online consumers guide to help you make good decisions.

UNIVERSITY HOSPITALS HOME PAGE
http://www.uhhs.com/
This site features an online health magazine covering pediatric and adult health issues. Want to see a topic covered? E-mail your request to the editor.

WOOD COUNTY HEALTH CARE SERVICES

http://www.wcnet.org/healthsvrs.html

This is community Internet at its best. The Wood County Health Department, Wood County Hospital, and local emergency services are all linked to this page, as well as health-related organizations in Wood County and links to health-related web sites.

WRIGHT STATE UNIVERSITY SCHOOL OF NURSING

http://www.nursing.wright.edu/resources/health.html

This nursing school home page has links to databases on topics ranging from AIDS to fibromyalgia to lupus.

XVI. Government

The Ohio state government has been at the forefront of getting Ohio online. The entire Ohio Revised Code is available electronically, as is the Ohio Administrative Code, both with keyword searching features. Ohio citizens are able to access the latest child support guidelines from their home computers, find out what the legislature did today, or listen to live reports from the Statehouse News Bureau. Ohio courts, political party home pages, contacts to state and local elected officials — you'll find it all here.

U.S. SENATE

DEWINE, MICHAEL
senator_dewine@dewine.senate.gov (e-mail)
http://www.senate.gov/~dewine/ (home page)

GLENN, JOHN
senator_glenn@glenn.senate.gov (e-mail)
http://little.nhlink.net/john-glenn/jglenn.htm (home page)

U.S. House of Representatives

http://www.geocities.com/CapitolHill/2817/congress.htm
If your representative is not here, check for any recent additions at the House of Representatives web e-mail listings address above. If your representative does not list an e-mail link, check the home page. Often there are forms within the page for sending e-mail messages.

Boehner, John
http://www.house.gov/boehner/ (home page)

Brown, Sherrod
sherrod@hr.house.gov (e-mail)

Gillmor, Paul
http://www.house.gov/gillmor (home page)

Hobson, David
http://www.house.gov/hobson/ (home page)

Hoke, Martin
HOKEMAIL@HR.HOUSE.GOV (e-mail)

Kaptur, Marcy
http://www.house.gov/kaptur/ (home page)

Kasich, John
http://www.house.gov/kasich/ (home page)

NEY, BOB

bobney@hr.house.gov (e-mail)
http://www.house.gov/ney/ (home page)

OXLEY, MICHAEL G.

oxley@hr.house.gov (e-mail)
http://www.house.gov/oxley/ (home page)

PORTMAN, ROB

portmail@hr.house.gov (e-mail)
http://www.house.gov/portman (home page)

PRYCE, DEBORAH

pryce15@hr.house.gov (e-mail)
http://www.house.gov/pryce (home page)

REGULA, RALPH

http://www.house.gov/regula/ (home page)

TRAFICANT, JAMES

telljim@hr.house.gov (e-mail)
http://www.house.gov/traficant/ (home page)

OHIO SENATE

http://www.knox.net/knox/govt/senate.htm *or*
http://www.knox.net/knox/govt/house.htm
If your senator or representative is not listed here, check these web sites for any updates.

Horn, Charles

sen.horn@ix.netcom.com (e-mail)

http://www.geocities.com/CapitolHill/2817 (home page)

Ohio House of Representatives

Amstutz, Ron

amstutz@pobox.com (e-mail)

http://www.bright.net/~ronams/ (home page)

Kasputis, Ed

http://www.kasputis.com/ (home page)

Terwilleger, George

gterwill@aol.com (e-mail)

http://www2.eos.net/ournet/GTERWILL (home page)

Williams, Bryan

http://www.bryanwilliams.com (home page)

Wise, Mike

mwise@ix.netcom.com (e-mail)

http://www.ofcn.org/mwise/ (home page)

Courthouses, State and Government Offices

Akron Municipal Court

http://www.neo.lrun.com:80/City_of_Akron/courts.html

Department phone numbers, organization, jurisdiction, location map, calendar, and list of judges are provided.

Athens City Council Home Page

http://www.seorf.ohiou.edu/~xx028

How cool for a tiny town like Athens to have their own web page for the city council. You can actually read city ordinances, both approved and proposed, online, as well as see a list of council members. And that's not all — visitors can e-mail the city council right from the web page.

Berea Municipal Court

http://clelaw.lib.oh.us/public/muni_ct/berea/homepage.htm

Rules of the court, plus a helpful section on how to file a small claim.

Bureau of Motor Vehicles

http://www.state.oh.us/odps/division/bmv/bmv.html

How and where to get an Ohio drivers license, styles and costs of Ohio license plates, plus information on agencies for each county.

BUREAU OF WORKERS COMPENSATION

http://www.ohiobwc.com/

How to file a claim, your rights, plus guidelines for new businesses.

CABINET MEMBERS

http://www.state.oh.us/gov/cabinet.html

Who's Director of Budget and Management, of Public Safety? How do you contact them? This is a list of the Governor's cabinet with links to their department web pages.

CHILLICOTHE MUNICIPAL COURT

http://www.bright.net/~bbutler

List of judges, rules, public records policy, and victim assistance program information.

COURT OF APPEALS OF OHIO EIGHTH APPELLATE DISTRICT

http://clelaw.lib.oh.us/public/homepgs/eighthom.htm

Ohio rules of appellate procedure, local rules of the court, list of judges, outline of the appellate process, plus answers to frequently asked questions.

CUYAHOGA COUNTY COURTS

http://clelaw.lib.oh.us/public/homepgs/cohome.htm#cocourts

Links to all county and municipal courts within Cuyahoga County. Sites include local rules, lists of judges, directions to the courthouse, and juror information.

DELAWARE COUNTY COURT OF COMMON PLEAS

http://www.co.delaware.oh.us/COURT/index.htm

Court rules, docket, and juror information, including online juror reporting confirmation.

FindLaw: Ohio

http://www.findlaw.com/11stategov/oh/

State code, constitution, session laws, court decisions, bill information, plus links to state government sites. This becomes an even more powerful site under subscription, but these main sites are available at no charge over the web.

Franklin County Court of Common Pleas

http://www.netwalk.com/~frankcty/courts/gen_div.htm

Links to court agencies, local rules, and dockets for each judge.

Governor's Home Page

http://www.state.oh.us/gov/

The Governor's biography, speeches, and announcements, plus links to his cabinet.

Hamilton County Juvenile Court

http://www.ncsc.dni.us/court/hamilton/homepage.htm

Court locations and list of services, along with a list of judges.

Internet Law Library-Ohio

http://law.house.gov/44.htm

Assembled by the U.S House of Representatives, this state page lists links to a wide variety of useful legal reference and governmental web sites, including the Ohio Revised Code, Ohio Supreme Court decisions, wildlife law, tax forms, and the U.S. Constitution. Of particular value are the summaries of consumer protection, firearms, public indecency, and medical malpractice laws in our state.

LIVING OHIO GOVERNMENT SERIES

http://www.logs.org/

A wonderful page intended for educators, this site discusses the process of Ohio government, links to free materials, museums, and other resources. The "Factoids" section highlights several impressive school projects concerning local history. Great information for students.

LUCAS COUNTY COURT OF COMMON PLEAS

http://commissioners.co.lucas.oh.us/a_elected-officials.html

Department phone numbers and list of judges.

MARIETTA MUNICIPAL COURT

http://ourworld.compuserve.com/homepages/marietta_muni_court

Recent decisions of the court are listed, as well as the current docket and online legal forms.

MONTGOMERY COUNTY COURT OF COMMON PLEAS

http://www.mccpc.montgomery.oh.us/

This is a great web page for county citizens, explaining the responsibilities of each court division and the procedure for obtaining information or filing suit within each subject area including adoption and marriage licenses.

NOLO PRESS SELF-HELP LAW CENTER

http://www.nolo.com

From the publishers of legal reference tools comes a current features section with daily tips, and articles written for the layman on common legal issues.

OHIO ADMINISTRATIVE CODE
http://204.89.181.223/oac.htm
The rules governing the agencies of the state of Ohio, searchable by keyword or table of contents.

OHIO ATTORNEY GENERAL OPINIONS
http://www.ag.ohio.gov/opinions/agopinio.htm
Beyond opinions, this site describes the functions of this office and includes an online consumer complaint form.

OHIO BUREAU OF EMPLOYMENT SERVICES
http://www.state.oh.us/obes/
Employment rates, labor market statistics, and most importantly, job listings from across the state.

OHIO CONSTITUTION
http://204.89.181.223/oconst.htm
The document in its entirety.

OHIO COURT RULES
http://204.89.181.223/ctrules.htm
The rules governing all courts of Ohio, essential to litigators.

OHIO DEMOCRATIC PARTY
http://www.democratic-party.org (Choose Ohio's state page)
Participate in an online discussion group on Ohio politics. Register to vote, join the party, or request an absentee ballot online. Check a political events calendar, radio broadcasts, and link to your county's Democratic Party home page.

OHIO DEPARTMENT OF ADMINISTRATIVE SERVICES

http://www.odn.ohio.gov/das/

This department serves as the business manager for Ohio. Included is information on obtaining a vendors license in the state.

OHIO DEPARTMENT OF AGRICULTURE

http://www.state.oh.us/agr/

Farmland preservation, commodity fact sheets, and water quality data, plus links to this year's county fair schedule.

OHIO DEPARTMENT OF ALCOHOL AND DRUG ADDICTION SERVICES

http://www.state.oh.us/ada/odada.htm

Find out what services are offered by the state, then link to county agencies for local service information.

OHIO DEPARTMENT OF COMMERCE

http://www.state.oh.us/commerce/

Lots of good information for businesses, plus a section for investors.

OHIO DEPARTMENT OF DEVELOPMENT

http://www.odod.ohio.gov/

Ohio Tourism with links to lots of great places to visit, plus an online export directory for Ohio business.

OHIO DEPARTMENT OF EDUCATION

http://www.ode.ohio.gov/

Statistics galore, including proficiency test results.

OHIO DEPARTMENT OF HEALTH

http://www.state.oh.us/doh/

Statistics on Ohio's health, plus publications, and a list of programs and services offered.

OHIO DEPARTMENT OF HUMAN SERVICES
http://www.state.oh.us/odhs/
Want to see who the most wanted child support offenders are? Their pictures are posted here.

OHIO DEPARTMENT OF INSURANCE
http://www.state.oh.us/ins/
Ohio Shoppers Guides to auto, home, long-term care, and Medicare supplement insurance are available here.

OHIO DEPARTMENT OF MENTAL HEALTH
http://www.mh.state.oh.us/

OHIO DEPARTMENT OF MENTAL RETARDATION AND DEVELOPMENTAL DISABILITIES
http://www.state.oh.us/dmr/

OHIO DEPARTMENT OF NATURAL RESOURCES
http://www.dnr.ohio.gov/
Hunting and fishing license information plus links to state parks and nature preserves. For agency web sites belonging to this department see the "Outdoors" chapter.

OHIO DEPARTMENT OF PUBLIC SAFETY
http://www.state.oh.us/odps/
Includes the Bureau of Motor Vehicles. For a direct link to this agency, see the address listed above.

OHIO DEPARTMENT OF REHABILITATION AND CORRECTIONS
http://www.drc.ohio.gov
Locations of state correctional facilities, including juvenile units, plus a drug tip hotline.

OHIO DEPARTMENT OF TAXATION
http://www.state.oh.us/tax

Forms and publications available for downloading, plus tax data series giving statistics on a variety of state tax revenues and rates by year and county.

OHIO DEPARTMENT OF TRANSPORTATION
http://www.dot.state.oh.us/

Where's the construction now and where is it going to be, plus what are those wildflowers growing in the median strips?

OHIO DIVORCE
http://www.divorceinfo.com/ohhelps.htm

This site provides summaries for many areas of Ohio divorce law including mediation and parental responsibilities, as well as a link to Ohio divorce frequently asked questions.

OHIO EPA
http://www.epa.ohio.gov/

Fact sheets, permits, and regulations, plus a list of hazardous waste sites across the state.

OHIO HOUSE DISTRICT MAP
http://www.logs.org/housemap.html

How useful. A quick glance at this map tells you the Ohio House district you live in.

OHIO LAW AND GOVERNMENT
http://www.lawresearch.com/csohi.htm

A very nice list of links to all three branches of Ohio government, developed for legal research purposes.

OHIO LEGAL INFORMATION CENTER

http://www.wwlia.org/usohhome.htm

Links to the Ohio Revised Code, and LAWeb, a list of Ohio lawyers and law firm web sites.

OHIO LEGAL RESOURCES

http://avv.com/orc

Direct links to the Ohio Revised Code, Ohio Session Law and the state of Ohio's home page.

OHIO OFFICE OF BUDGET AND MANAGEMENT

http://www.state.oh.us/obm

If you're wondering just where our tax money goes, the state budget is available from this web site, both in summary and in real dollars and cents.

OHIO REPUBLICAN PARTY

http://www.ohiogop.org

County organizations information and links to Ohio congressional and executive republicans.

OHIO REVISED CODE

http://38.223.23.20/stacks/orc/

The codified law of the State of Ohio, searchable by keyword, title number, or subject category.

OHIO RIGHT TO LIFE HOME PAGE

http://www.ohiolife.org/

One of the most active political groups in Ohio hosts an extensive web site, linking to many court cases and articles of interest to the cause.

OHIO SECRETARY OF STATE

http://www.state.oh.us/sos

Voter registration information and upcoming election dates.

OHIO SENATE DISTRICTS

http://www.logs.org/senmap.html

A very useful map showing all 88 Ohio counties and the senate district numbers that coincide.

OHIO SESSION LAW

http://38.223.23.20/stacks/ohioacts/

Before a law that the legislature has passed makes it into the Ohio Revised Code, it is part of Session Law. If you're looking for a law that you know has recently been passed, check here. Searchable by keyword, House or Senate Bill numbers, or ORC title number.

PUBLIC UTILITIES COMMISSION OF OHIO

http://mabel.puc.ohio.gov/

This watchdog agency posts press releases on its home page to keep Ohioans abreast of the latest hearings. The complaint process is explained for those wishing to file a grievance with the commission.

STATE AUDITOR'S OFFICE

http://www.auditor.ohio.gov/auditor/

This is about as close as you want to get to this department! What they do, in great detail, can be found here.

STATE TREASURER'S OFFICE

http://www.state.oh.us/treasurer

Many people wonder if they unwittingly are owed millions from Unclaimed Funds. Here's where to find out.

STATE OF OHIO FRONT PAGE

http://www.ohio.gov/ohio/index.htm

If you're looking for an Ohio government department or agency, this site has links to them all.

STATEHOUSE NEWS BUREAU

http://www.tcom.ohiou.edu/opr/

Put together by the Ohio Public Radio, this site offers radio broadcasts over the Internet of up to the minute news from the Statehouse, plus replays of radio broadcasts on hot political topics. If you've got RealAudio, you're on your way to some of the best news reporting in the state.

SUPREME COURT OF OHIO

http://www.sconet.ohio.gov

Read court announcements and opinions, get Bar Exam results, access addresses on topics given by our Chief Justice, and, best of all, follow major court cases as they happen.

TOLL-FREE DIRECTORY FOR STATE AGENCIES

http://www.state.oh.us/slg/800nos.htm

UNCLAIMED FUNDS

http://www.state.oh.us/com/ucf

Ever get that feeling someone owes you something? Check this web site — it could be true.

U.S. Court of Appeals Sixth Circuit

http://www.law.emory.edu/6circuit

Lists decisions by the court over the past three years, searchable by keyword.

U.S. District Court for the Northern District of Ohio

http://www.ohnd.uscourts.gov/

Local rules governing bankruptcy, civil, and criminal trials.

Voter's First Project

http://votersfirst.wksu.kent.edu/

Local race results, candidates and issues for Northeastern Ohio compiled by the local public radio station.

Winslo

http://winslo.ohio.gov

This World Wide Web information network from the State Library of Ohio links visitors to all departments and agencies of Ohio government, plus the online catalog of the State Library.

XVII. Travel

Travel down the "Ohighway" to Ohio state park resorts, bed and breakfasts, plus county and state tourism web sites. Link to road conditions, and check a special list of speed traps before you set out on your Ohio adventure.

The Amish and the Plain People

http://www.800padutch.com/amish.html

This site provides great background information about the Amish and Mennonites. Set up in a question and answer format, the history, dress, language, customs, and education of these "plain people" are discussed. If you have a question not answered within this web site, you may e-mail it to the site's host, and they will post the answer on the site.

Amish Heartland

http://www.amish-heartland.com

This site highlights local events, attractions, and restaurants, provides maps of Holmes and surrounding counties, and features articles reflecting local culture. Local weather conditions and construction information are provided for Ohio travelers.

CLEVELAND AREA BED AND BREAKFASTS
http://www.apk.net/cleveland/lifestyle/bedbreak/
This is a listing of all bed and breakfasts in the Cleveland area with web pages. A link is provided to each inn's site for further description and reservation information.

ERIE COUNTY VISITORS AND CONVENTION BUREAU
http://www.buckeyenorth.com/
If you've ever seen a copy of Buckeye North Magazine, you know what's in store for you here — lots of beautiful pictures and tourist stops from the northern Ohio shores.

GREENE COUNTY CONVENTION AND VISITORS BUREAU
http://www.greenecountyohio.org/
Minutes from Dayton lies this serene farmland dotted with quaint small towns. Visit this web site to preview points of interest, festivals and events, accommodations, or contact the bureau for further information.

HOLMES COUNTY TOURIST INFORMATION AND RESOURCE CENTER
http://www.visitamishcountry.com
In addition to an overview of the county, this site highlights the large Amish population, including information on safely and courteously sharing the road with horse-drawn buggies. With links to bed and breakfasts and local businesses, including flea markets and antique shops, this site heavily promotes the tourist opportunities in Amish country.

HOTWIRED ROUGH GUIDE-OHIO
http://www.hotwired.com/rough/usa/great.lakes/ohio/index.html
Posted by the editors of the Rough Guide Travel series, this site is great for tourists, with links to food, hotels, and night life, but only covers Cincinnati and Cleveland at this time.

THE INN AT CEDAR FALLS

http://www.innatcedarfalls.com/

Wouldn't it be nice to know exactly what you're getting ahead of time when booking a hotel reservation? If you're staying at this inn near Hocking Hills, you can preview the rooms, outdoor and indoor eating areas, and the beauty of the surrounding area online, then e-mail your reservation.

INNS AND B&Bs IN OHIO

http://www.inns.com/midwest/ai-oh.htm

If small inns and quaint bed and breakfasts are your choice for accommodations, this site will link you to a list for every area in Ohio you may be traveling through, together with price, accessibility and rules concerning children.

LAKE COUNTY VISITORS BUREAU

http://www.lakevisit.com/

Close to Cleveland but rural enough to be called a mini Napa Valley, Lake County boasts an annual walleye tournament, wineries, golf, and Ohio's longest beach. Check this site for details.

LORAIN COUNTY VISITORS BUREAU

http://www.lcvb.org/

This beautiful site will surely lure you to Lorain County. Before you go, check online information on lodging, shopping, dining, birding, special attractions, and prime fishing spots.

MARKKO VINEYARD

http://www.markko.com/

Part of the flavor of the Lake Erie shore is the vineyards. This web site describes one of those vineyards, and includes a wine list, calendar of events, and directions to the winery.

MIDWEST LIVING'S OHIO PAGE

http://www.midwestliving.com/goodbets/ohio.html

The magazine's list of events, lodging, restaurants, and "good bets" for the state of Ohio.

OHIGHWAY

http://www.ohighway.com/right.html

Link to community and visitor information for the East Central Ohio area.

OHIO AMISH COUNTRY VISITORS GUIDE

http://www.kramer.com/ohio-amish-country/index.html

Published by Graphics Publications, this site includes a visitor's guide, maps, event calendar, plus traffic safety tips.

OHIO ROAD CONDITIONS

http://www.dot.state.oh.us/cond.htm

Next time you're wondering whether to venture forth through a winter storm, check this Department of Transportation web site for advice about road conditions. Includes construction information for the rest of the year.

OHIO SPEEDTRAPS

http://www.speedtrap.com/speedtrap/ohio.html

Wonder what law enforcement thinks of this site? Choose from the metropolitan area you'll be traveling through or go to the miscellaneous link for small towns to see where the radar hot spots are located. A "new traps" listing gives you current additions not found in the regular links.

OHIO STATE PARK RESORTS

http://www.tw-rec-resorts.com/

Definitely some of the nicest places to stay, especially for families, with plenty of nature nearby. This site tells you where they are and provides links to each one for more detailed information.

OTTAWA COUNTY VISITORS BUREAU

http://www.lake-erie.com/

Port Clinton, Put-In-Bay, Lakeside, and Marblehead attractions are featured on this site.

PUT-IN-BAY ISLAND GUIDE

http://www.put-in-bay.com/

Boating, shopping, dining, attractions, accommodations, and fishing information for the Lake Erie Island region are all included, as well as summer job information and an island guide map.

RIVERTOWNS IN THE HEART OF THE MID-OHIO VALLEY

http://www.rivertowns.org/

This page posted by the Marietta/Washington County Convention and Visitors Bureau includes dining, shopping, and lodging links, plus a local calendar of events.

SANDUSKY COUNTY

http://www.sandusky-county.org/tourist-info/
Things to do, special events, maps, calendar of events, lodging, plus a monthly online feature.

TRAVEL.OHIO!

http://www.ohiotourism.com/
This is the official site of the Ohio Department of Travel and Tourism and is a one-stop shopping site for Ohio travel information. In addition to lodging, and attractions, there is a featured site with more in-depth information about a particular place or event. The event section allows you to pick a month and city, then read what events are scheduled in that area for that time period.

WARREN COUNTY

http://ww2.ohio4fun.org/ohio4fun
With Kings Island entertainment, Lebanon history, and lots of outdoor spaces, this site has a lot to talk about. Link to shopping, festivals, sports, bed and breakfasts, and dining information.

WAYNE COUNTY CONVENTION AND VISITORS BUREAU

http://www.wooster-wayne.com/wccvb/
Wayne County is beautiful, rolling farmland in the heart of Amish country. Check this site to preview intriguing places, shopping, arts, and accommodations.

ZANESVILLE/MUSKINGUM COUNTY TOURISM

http://www.zanesville-ohio.com/ZCC/tourism.htm
Things to do, shopping, attractions, parks, restaurants, and golf courses for the Zanesville area.

XVIII. Maps

At first glance, you might think maps belong in the travel section. Once you visit the sites included in this chapter, you'll see that maps are a lot more than papers that get you from point A to point B. The Cleveland Public Library and Cleveland State University have put together terrific map catalogs that will show you geography, geology, transportation, and history, along with standard city and road maps.

CLEVELAND CARTOGRAPHY
http://www.csuohio.edu/CUT/Clevmaps.htm
Maintained by Cleveland State University, this large site links to cartographers, marine and aviation charts, map dealers and publishers, weather maps, and geography departments at Ohio universities.

CLEVELAND PUBLIC LIBRARY MAP COLLECTION
http://www.cpl.org/010036/010036CLEVELAND.SHTML
The best online collection for maps in Ohio, this site contains links to Cleveland, state-wide, historical, and geological maps plus links to other map collections nationwide.

CLEVELAND WEATHER MAP

http://www.csuohio.edu/nws/

Choose from Cleveland Doplar radar, daily climate information, regional surface plots, or daily weather trivia.

GREAT LAKES DEMOGRAPHIC SERVER

http://sedac.ciesin.org/plue/ddviewer/htmls/map-gtlk.html

Choose from a menu of options to create maps for the state or individual counties depicting up to 25 demographic variables, including land area in square miles, percent population by race, gender, age or income level, rural and farm populations, or population density.

GREAT LAKES MAP SERVER

http://epawww.ciesin.org/arc/map-home.html

This map server allows users to interactively compose a map for any area within the Great Lakes region.

HOW FAR IS IT?

http://www.indo.com/distance

Enter two cities and this database calculates the distance between them. It also prints a map showing the two places.

MAPQUEST

http://www.mapquest.com/

Although not specific to Ohio, this site is terrific for printing personalized travel maps. It offers the unique feature of printing out driving directions, something that's often more useful than a printed map. Choose between shortest distance or fastest speed between any two addresses.

MAPS FOR OHIO CITIES

http://www.carhire.com/maps/oh.html

These are maps that car rental companies offer as one-time, one-copy downloads. Major cities only.

NEIGHBORHOOD LINK

http://little.nhlink.net/nhlink/image/maps/map.htm

Shows boundaries of Cleveland neighborhoods, plus voting wards and social service agencies within each area.

NORTHERN OHIO DATA AND INFORMATION SERVICE (NODIS)

http://cua6.csuohio.edu/~ucweb/nodis/gis/nodisgis.htm

A Gallery of maps includes land use in Cuyahoga county, manufacturing employment in Cuyahoga county, city of Barberton zoning districts, and toxic chemical release sites.

OHIO GEOLOGIC MAPS

http://www.uakron.edu/geology/ohioMaps/ohmaps.html

Maintained by the University of Akron, these maps show Ohio glacial deposits, bedrock geology, Ohio soil regions, and ground-water resources.

OHIO PROFILES

http://www.census.gov/datamap/www/39.html

Select a county on this Ohio map and receive corresponding U.S. census statistics.

OHIO WEBSITE LOCATOR

http://www.zygaena.com/ohio/index.html

Click on an area of an Ohio map and this site will list links to all the web sites in that area. Currently maps only large metropolitan areas.

XIX. Outdoors

Camping, hunting, and fishing regulations for this season are online in Ohio. Natural caves and caverns, national forests, state parks, and city gardens all have their own home pages. The Ohio Department of Natural Resources offers its publications online and lists which wildlife is currently visible in each area of the state.

Adams Lake State Park
http://www.dnr.ohio.gov/odnr/parks/directory/adams.htm
Description and history of the park, phone numbers for park offices, and availability of fishing, boating, and trails.

Alum Creek State Park
http://www.dnr.ohio.gov/odnr/parks/directory/alum.htm
Boating, fishing, and swimming regulations, phone numbers for park offices, plus information on area attractions.

Audubon Ohio
http://www.audubon.org/chapter/oh/index.html
This site lists chapters of the Audubon Society within Ohio and links to those with web pages.

A.W. MARION STATE PARK

http://www.dnr.ohio.gov/odnr/parks/directory/awmarin.htm

Good description of the park itself plus contact points for any other information you may be lacking, including an e-mail contact for the Department of Natural Resources.

BARKCAMP STATE PARK

http://www.dnr.ohio.gov/odnr/parks/directory/barkcamp.htm

Visitors to this Belmont park will be able to fully plan ahead — history and description, park contacts, plus recreational opportunities are all included.

BEAVER CREEK STATE PARK

http://www.dnr.ohio.gov/odnr/parks/directory/beaverck.htm

Wild and scenic Little Beaver Creek, which traverses this park, provides a great opportunity to ride the rapids. Visit this home page to find out about boating, camping, picnicking, plus a great description of the breathtaking scenery.

BLUE ROCK STATE PARK

http://www.dnr.ohio.gov/odnr/parks/directory/bluerock.htm

This lovely park in central Ohio hosts a home page with all the information you'll need to plan a great visit.

BOWLING GREEN CITY PARKS

http://www.wcnet.org/Art_Culture/parks/bgcityparks.html

What can you do at each of Bowling Green's city parks? This site tells you where you can sled, where the tennis courts are, and which parks have playground and picnic facilities.

BUCK CREEK STATE PARK

http://www.dnr.ohio.gov/odnr/parks/directory/buckck.htm

Planning a trip to Springfield? This home page describes the scenery awaiting you at Buck Creek. Fishing, picnicking, and trail information, plus contact numbers for park personnel.

BUCKEYE LAKE STATE PARK

http://www.dnr.ohio.gov/odnr/parks/directory/buckeye.htm

Home of the oldest state park in Ohio, this page lists recreational opportunities like swimming, skiing and boating, history and description of the natural area, plus contact information for park offices.

BURR OAK STATE PARK

http://www.dnr.ohio.gov/odnr/parks/directory/burroak.htm

One of eight state parks with a lodge, this site lists what you can do, what you can see, where you can stay, and who you can contact for more information.

CAESAR CREEK STATE PARK

http://www.dnr.ohio.gov/odnr/parks/directory/caesarck.htm

Fishing, boating, hiking and contact information for park offices, plus a good description of the natural area.

CATAWBA ISLAND

http://www.dnr.ohio.gov/odnr/parks/directory/LAKEERIE.htm

Ah, the wonder of the Lake Erie islands. This page describes nearby attractions, island geography, and links to other nearby natural areas.

CLEVELAND LAKEFRONT STATE PARK

http://www.dnr.ohio.gov/odnr/parks/directory/clevelkf.htm

On the edge of the inner city lies the shore of magnificent Lake Erie. Recreational activities and contact points for the park are included on this home page.

COLUMBUS AUDUBON SOCIETY

http://www.geography.ohio-state.edu/CAS/

Membership information, plus a list of activities, current projects, officers, and statement of purpose.

COWAN LAKE STATE PARK

http://www.dnr.ohio.gov/odnr/parks/directory/cowanlk.htm

Located near Wilmington, this park hosts a home page listing hours, park personnel, description of the natural area, plus recreational opportunities.

COX ARBORETUM-DAYTON

http://aabga.mobot.org/AABGA/Member.pages/cox.arb.html

Special collections, seasonal displays as well as location and hours are featured.

CRANE CREEK STATE PARK

http://www.dnr.ohio.gov/odnr/parks/directory/cranecrk.htm

Noted for its bird watching, this natural area along the Lake Erie shore hosts a home page describing the wildlife available for sighting, the freshwater marshes and sandy shores.

CUYAHOGA VALLEY NATIONAL RECREATION AREA

http://www.nps.gov./cuva

Truly a gem lying between the urban sprawl of Akron and Cleveland, CVNRA offers a wide range of recreational opportunities. This web site gives good advice about seasonal recommended clothing, accessibility, recommended park use, length of stay, and lodging and camping facilities. Visitor center exhibits, programs and activities are listed, as are trails and roads that run through the park. CVNRA offers a program for educators called "Teaching with Historic Places" that helps students understand how parks relate to American historical experience and cultural expression. Information on this lesson plan can be found at the CVNRA web site.

DAVIS MEMORIAL

http://www.oplin.lib.oh.us/OHS2/site/sites/southwest/davis.html

Located in Adams County, this scenic preserve includes dolomite cliffs, a cave, and hiking trails. Visit the online site for a description of the area and its flora, plus location information.

DAWES ARBORETUM-NEWARK

http://www.dawesarb.org

Read research reports, guides to available programs, and view photographs of the arboretum.

DAYTON AUDUBON SOCIETY

http://www.dayton.net/Audubon/

Read the chapter's newsletter online, check the field trip and events schedules, locate Dayton area birding sites and find out which species have been spotted lately.

DEER CREEK STATE PARK

http://www.dnr.ohio.gov/odnr/parks/directory/deercrk.htm

Located near Mt. Sterling in south-central Ohio, this is one of eight state parks with a lodge. Check this web site for contact information concerning lodging, plus boating, fishing and hiking information.

DELAWARE STATE PARK

http://www.dnr.ohio.gov/odnr/parks/directory/delaware.htm

Just north of Columbus lies refuge from the pavement and shopping malls. Check this web site to see what recreational opportunities await.

DILLON STATE PARK

http://www.dnr.ohio.gov/odnr/parks/directory/dillon.htm

Located near Nashport in Muskingum County, this park's home page includes a good description of the natural area plus hiking, camping, boating, and cabin availability.

EAST FORK STATE PARK

http://www.dnr.ohio.gov/odnr/parks/directory/eastfork.htm

One of the largest Ohio state parks, East Fork is located 25 miles from Cincinnati and hosts a home page including boating, fishing, camping and hiking information.

EAST HARBOR STATE PARK

http://www.dnr.ohio.gov/odnr/parks/directory/eharbor.htm

Noted for its shorebirds and waterfowl, this state park's site includes camping, boating, and swimming information, plus contacts to park personnel.

FELLOWS RIVERSIDE GARDENS-YOUNGSTOWN

http://www.neont.com/millck/frgarden.htm

Visiting this lovely web site is the next best thing to being there. Take a virtual tour, then check the calendar of events to plan your visit.

FINDLEY STATE PARK

http://www.dnr.ohio.gov/odnr/parks/directory/findley.htm

Located near Wellington, this park's home page has all the information you need — boating, fishing and camping information, plus contact numbers for park offices.

FORKED RUN STATE PARK

http://www.dnr.ohio.gov/odnr/parks/directory/forkedrn.htm

In addition to the usual address and phone numbers for park offices, this site has a wonderful description of the natural area plus the fish and game native to the area.

FRANKLIN PARK CONSERVATORY-COLUMBUS

http://www.physics.ohio-state.edu/~discover/Guide/conservatory.html

This web site serves as part of the curriculum for local schools. Beyond the usual information, there is a downloadable activity to do while you visit the garden.

GENEVA STATE PARK

http://www.dnr.ohio.gov/odnr/parks/directory/geneva.htm

Located on the northeast shore of Lake Erie, this park hosts a site describing the sandy beaches, marshes and estuaries and listing contact points for park offices.

GRAND LAKE ST. MARY'S STATE PARK

http://www.dnr.ohio.gov/odnr/parks/directory/grndlake.htm

Within Mercer County lies a large lake within a state park. This home page includes boating, fishing, swimming, and other recreational opportunities as well as links to other natural local attractions.

GREAT SEAL STATE PARK

http://www.dnr.ohio.gov/odnr/parks/directory/grtseal.htm

The steep hills found in this park are depicted on the Great Seal of Ohio — thence it's name. This web site offers information on the rugged terrain, plus advice for hikers and park contact information.

GREATER AKRON AUDUBON SOCIETY

http://www.cs.uakron.edu/~pelz/gaas.html

This page is loaded with information on topics such as wildlife rehabilitation and annual bird counts, along with society programs such as traveling displays, Audubon Adventure, Armchair Activist, and the Books in Schools Program.

GUILFORD LAKE STATE PARK

http://www.dnr.ohio.gov/odnr/parks/directory/guilford.htm

Located in northeast Ohio, this state park centers around a peaceful fishing lake. Its home page offers advice for hikers, picnickers, and other nature enthusiasts, while giving a nice description of the area's natural flora and fauna.

HARRISON LAKE STATE PARK

http://www.dnr.ohio.gov/odnr/parks/directory/harrison.htm

Canoeing, camping, fishing, swimming — read all about what this park near Fayette has to offer.

HEADLANDS BEACH STATE PARK

http://www.dnr.ohio.gov/odnr/parks/directory/headlands.htm

Boasting the largest natural sand beach in the state, this park's web site lists the various recreational opportunities, plus area natural attractions.

HOCKING HILLS INTERNET GUIDE

http://www.hockinghills.com

"Southern Ohio's Scenic Wonderland" has a wonderful website that gives separate treatment to each area of the 9000-acre preserve. Included is a discussion of the preserve's ecology, a map of the area, a photo gallery, plus information on nearby Lake Logan and Lake Hope. "Ways and Wanderings" highlights native flora and fauna, and even offers recipes. "Trail Notes" includes updates and visitor comments. "Of a Creative Nature" features short stories, artwork, poems, history, and musings celebrating the beauty of the area. Truly a comprehensive site emphasizing the awe-inspiring splendor of Hocking Hills.

HOLDEN ARBORETUM-KIRTLAND

http://www.holdenarb.org

In addition to beautiful gardens, this arboretum has a large library. The web site describes the collection, current research projects, and conservation efforts. Landscape consulting is offered, as well as links to other horticultural and botanical web sites. The ranger page includes pictures of the arboretum, the wildlife found there, and a location map.

HUESTON WOODS STATE PARK

http://www.dnr.ohio.gov/odnr/parks/directory/huestonw.htm

Located near the Indiana border in southwestern Ohio, Hueston Woods is one of eight Ohio state parks that includes a lodge. A large lake within the park provides opportunities for water sports. This site describes all these opportunities plus the wildlife rehabilitation center located here.

HUNTING AND FISHING LICENSE INFORMATION

http://www.dnr.state.oh.us/odnr/wildlife/license.html

Permit fees for all types of hunting, both resident and non-resident, dates the licenses are valid, and issuing agencies.

INDEPENDENCE DAM STATE PARK

http://www.dnr.ohio.gov/odnr/parks/directory/indpndam.htm

Along the banks of the Maumee River near Defiance lies this lovely state park. Visit its web site to read about camping, fishing, boating, and canoeing opportunities, plus the park office address and phone numbers.

INDIAN LAKE STATE PARK

http://www.dnr.ohio.gov/odnr/parks/directory/indianlk.htm
This center for fishing near Lakeview hosts a web page describing the natural area and recreational opportunities available.

JACKSON LAKE STATE PARK

http://www.dnr.ohio.gov/odnr/parks/directory/jacksonl.htm
Nestled near Oak Hill, this park's main attraction is a peaceful fishing lake. Read about the natural history of the area, what kind of wildlife lives here, and what facilities the park offers.

JEFFERSON LAKE STATE PARK

http://www.dnr.ohio.gov/odnr/parks/directory/jefferso.htm
This site describes the wonderful recreation available at this lovely park near Richmond, as well as the natural history of the area.

JOHN BRYAN STATE PARK

http://www.dnr.ohio.gov/odnr/parks/directory/jhnbryan.htm
The limestone gorge in this park near Yellow Springs is well worth the trip. Read how the gorge was formed, then find out about camping and other local natural attractions.

KELLEY'S ISLAND

http://www.dnr.ohio.gov/odnr/parks/directory/LAKEERIE.htm
Anyone who has taken a leisurely bike ride along the shores of this peaceful island knows how refreshing a day here can be. Check out this web site to learn about Kelley's natural history, family activities, and local attractions.

KINGWOOD CENTER-MANSFIELD

http://www.richnet.net/richland/attract/kingwood.html
This 47-acre public garden's web site hosts a picture archive of its lovely landscaping and historic Kingwood Hall.

KISER LAKE STATE PARK

http://www.dnr.ohio.gov/odnr/parks/directory/kisrlake.htm
Picture a peaceful sailing lake amid the wooded hills near Rosewood. Then go to this web site to learn about the natural history, swimming and fishing areas, and hiking trails waiting for you here.

KROHN CONSERVATORY-CINCINNATI

http://cinci.com/recreation/parks/krohn/krohn.html
Take a virtual tour of this "rainforest under glass," check special events, and visit the butterfly page.

LAKE ALMA STATE PARK

http://www.dnr.ohio.gov/odnr/parks/directory/LAKEALMA.htm
This peaceful lake near Wellston offers great fishing and camping. Learn about the flora and fauna found here, read a description of the natural area, check camping facilities, or contact park officials.

LAKE HOPE STATE PARK

http://www.dnr.ohio.gov/odnr/parks/directory/LAKEHOPE.htm
Nestled near Hocking Hills, this park's web site describes the recreational opportunities offered here, highlighting its unique stone lodge.

Lake Logan State Park

http://www.dnr.ohio.gov/odnr/parks/directory/LKLOGAN.htm

This day park near Hocking Hills has a wonderful web site describing the natural area and the recreational opportunities awaiting you.

Lake Loramie State Park

http://www.dnr.ohio.gov/odnr/parks/directory/LKLORAME.htm

Traveling near Minster anytime soon? Check this web site for the outstanding outdoor adventure opportunities available at this beautiful state park, then e-mail ODNR for additional information.

Lake Milton State Park

http://www.dnr.ohio.gov/odnr/parks/directory/LKMILTON.htm

If you love water sports, check this web site for information on the skiing, boating and fishing opportunities available at this large reservoir in northeast Ohio.

Lake White State Park

http://www.dnr.ohio.gov/odnr/parks/directory/LKWHITEW.htm

The great outdoors comes alive at this beautiful park near Waverly and the web site tells you the what, where and when of it all.

Little Miami State and National Scenic River

http://www.dnr.ohio.gov/odnr/parks/directory/LILMIAMI.htm

This wild and exciting river extends 105 miles, 86 of which are canoeable. Read about this incredible natural area, its dangers and thrills, the 50-mile Miami trail that follows it, and camping opportunities along its path.

MT. AIRY ARBORETUM-CINCINNATI

http://cinci.com/recreation/parks/text/mtairy.html
This landscape arboretum is made up of small demonstration gardens nestled within an urban forest. Check this web site for a description of this 120 acre site.

MT. GILEAD STATE PARK

http://www.dnr.ohio.gov/odnr/parks/directory/MTGILEAD.htm
This small fishing and hiking area in central Ohio has a great home page describing the natural area, history of the region, and outdoor activities available there.

MADISON LAKE STATE PARK

http://www.dnr.ohio.gov/odnr/parks/directory/MADISON.htm
This peaceful natural area is just right for those who crave a more relaxed setting. Visit this web page to read about boating restrictions, picnic areas, plus the flora and fauna of the surrounding forest.

MARY JANE THURSTON STATE PARK

http://www.dnr.ohio.gov/odnr/parks/directory/MJTHRSTN.htm
This unique park along the shores of the Maumee River hosts a web page filled with information about the area's natural history, historic remnants of canal days, and the great stream fishing available here.

MAUMEE BAY STATE PARK

http://www.dnr.ohio.gov/odnr/parks/directory/MAUMEBAY.htm
Along the northwest coast of Lake Erie lies this large all-inclusive state park. Visit its web site to read about the opportunities for outdoor sportsmen, naturalists, or those simply seeking some rest and relaxation.

MOHICAN STATE PARK

http://www.dnr.ohio.gov/odnr/parks/directory/MOHICAN.htm

Located near Loudonville, this is prime camping, canoeing, and hiking country. Check this site for nearby attractions plus information about Mohican's beautiful lodge and winter recreational opportunities.

MOSQUITO LAKE STATE PARK

http://www.dnr.ohio.gov/odnr/parks/directory/MOSQUITO.htm

With a name like Mosquito Lake, this must be a very small place, right? Wrong. Mosquito Lake is actually one of the largest lakes in Ohio. Visit this web site to learn how this area got its name, and what fun is waiting for you there.

NELSON KENNEDY LEDGES

http://www.dnr.ohio.gov/odnr/parks/directory/NELSONK.htm

These rugged cliffs offer gorgeous views, picnicking, and hiking. Check the web site for location, park office information, and hours of operation.

OHIO BIOLOGICAL SURVEY

http://www-obs.biosci.ohio-state.edu

Want to know what species of ants, spiders, mammals, or birds live in Ohio? This is the website for you. This group from 76 Ohio colleges, universities, museums, state agencies, and others collects statistics on all the species native to Ohio. Great site for school reports.

OHIO BIRDER RESOURCES

http://www.bright.net/~vfazio/avesohio.htm

Where to find birds in Ohio, species counts, Ohio birding organizations, plus statewide bird activities are featured. There is a virtual field guide, or "image library" at this site, plus range maps for all Ohio species.

OHIO BOATING LAWS

http://www.dnr.state.oh.us/odnr/watercraft/laws/laws.html

Operator laws, required equipment, state park regulations, plus fishing regulations.

OHIO CAVERNS

http://www.cavern.com/ohiocaverns

View the cave map before you go, get directions, and visit the cavern store online. These caverns, touted as "Ohio's Outstanding Natural Wonder" are located in West Liberty, Ohio, and have been open for tours for over 100 years.

OHIO DEPARTMENT OF NATURAL RESOURCES

http://www.dnr.ohio.gov

This large department overlooks many natural resource divisions, including the ones listed below. Start from the ODNR homepage, or go directly to the divisions that deal with your topic. Check the calendar of events for special events planned in Ohio's state parks. Hunting, boating, and fishing regulations are governed by this division and have been listed as separate sites for your convenience.

OHIO DIVISION OF FORESTRY

http://www.hcs.ohio-state.edu/ODNR/Forestry.htm

This is a wonderful site for anyone interested in forestry. Wildfire statistics, rainfall maps, forest diseases, insects, stresses, and health are discussed, along with special reports on Buckeye trees and gypsy moths. State forest descriptions, recreational information and events are included.

OHIO DIVISION OF NATURAL AREAS AND PRESERVES

http://www.dnr.ohio.gov/odnr/dnap/dnap.html

Links to Ohio natural arches, riparian birds, detailed information on the fishes native to Ohio's scenic rivers, and an online preserve access permit request form.

OHIO DIVISION OF OIL AND GAS

http://www.dnr.state.oh.us/odnr/oil+gas

This is a useful site for anyone reaping oil or gas from her own land. There is a county inspector locator map, a list of regional offices, and chapters from the Ohio Revised Code and Ohio Administrative Code concerning oil and gas law.

OHIO DIVISION OF WILDLIFE

http://www.dnr.state.oh.us/odnr/wildlife/wildlife.html

Ohio watchable wildlife sites are listed for each region of the state, plus information on wildlife diversity, a wildlife calendar, list of division publications, and, as an added bonus to Ohio hunters, venison and fish recipes.

OHIO ENDANGERED SPECIES LIST

http://www.fws.gov/~r9endspp/statl-r3.html#LnkOH
This list, put out by U.S. Fish and Wildlife Service, is one frequently requested for school reports. Students, keep this URL handy.

OHIO GEOLOGICAL SURVEY

http://www.dnr.state.oh.us/odnr/geo_survey
Geofacts, downloadable screen size geologic maps, information on fossils and minerals, Lake Erie facts and history, plus energy and mineral statistics, and coal and petroleum reserves by county.

OHIO OUTDOORS

http://ezines.firelands.net/OhioOutdoors/
This online version of the hunting magazine by the same name not only has regular featured articles, but links to other hunting web sites from its home page.

OHIO STATE SCENIC RIVERS

http://www.dnr.ohio.gov/odnr/dnap/sr/srivers.html
Each of the ten rivers designated scenic in Ohio are described in detail, including the fishes native to them. This site has beautiful photography and good ecosystem information.

OHIO WILDFLOWER PROGRAM

http://www.dot.state.oh.us/wildfl.htm
Ever wonder what those beautiful flowers growing in the median strips are called? This page, put out by the Ohio Department of Transportation, lets you click on each wildflower picture to get a species' name.

OLENTANGY INDIAN CAVERNS

http://www.goodearth.com/showcave/oh/olentangy.html

A history of the caverns north of Columbus, plus tour information, area sites of interest, Ohio Frontier Land, a recreation of a frontier town in Indian country, and nearby Indian Museum. Download a map to the caverns from this site.

PAINT CREEK STATE PARK

http://www.dnr.ohio.gov/odnr/parks/directory/PAINTCRK.htm

Paint Creek might sound tiny, but it actually has a large lake, camping, plus Paint Creek Pioneer Farm, a restored historical farm from the 1800's. Check the web site for hours of operation, plus recreational opportunities available within this lovely park.

PERRY'S CAVE

http://isis.infinet.com/thecave

Called the "greatest site under the island," this cave is located in Put-In-Bay, South Bass Island. Enter the virtual cave entrance for the cave's history plus admission hours and fees.

PIKE LAKE STATE PARK

http://www.dnr.ohio.gov/odnr/parks/directory/PIKELAKE.htm

Check this web site for natural history and recreational opportunities within this park surrounded by state forest in central Ohio.

PORTAGE LAKES STATE PARK

http://wwww.dnr.ohio.gov/odnr/parks/directory/PORTAGE.htm

A series of lakes and wetlands hosting shorebirds and waterfowl, this park south of Akron has a nice web page describing the natural area, boating regulations, and camping facilities.

PUNDERSON STATE PARK

http://www.dnr.ohio.gov/odnr/parks/directory/PUNDRSON.htm

This large park, complete with lodge and golf course, is a great place for winter sports. Visit the web page for details on hotel amenities, course features, recreational opportunities, plus local attractions.

PYMATUNING STATE PARK

http://www.dnr.ohio.gov/odnr/parks/directory/PYMATUNG.htm

Walleye fishermen take note. This park located near Andover claims to have one of the finest walleye fishing lakes in the country. Check its web site for details on this and other available outdoor opportunities plus park history and contact numbers.

PUT-IN-BAY FISHING GUIDE

http://www.put-in-bay.com/fishing.htm

Find out where the fish are each season in the waters surrounding South Bass Island. Fishing limits are posted, as well as license requirements, and prime spots for each species.

QUAIL HOLLOW STATE PARK

http://www.dnr.ohio.gov/odnr/parks/directory/QUAILHLW.htm

Surrounding a 40-room manor are gardens, hiking trails, and cross country skiing opportunities. This web page will tell you the history of the manor, the park, and what seasonal opportunities and events are planned at this site near Hartville.

ROCKY FORK STATE PARK

http://www.dnr.ohio.gov/odnr/parks/directory/ROCKYFRK.htm

Wetlands, gorges and caves abound in this large state park near Hillsboro. Visit its web site to learn about the natural area, nearby attractions, and water sports available on the large inland lake.

SALT FORK STATE PARK

http://www.dnr.ohio.gov/odnr/parks/directory/SALTFORK.htm

This wonderful natural area near Cambridge boasts a large lake for boating, camping and fishing, hundreds of woodland acres for hiking, plus a golf course and lodge. Visit this web site to learn more about the natural area, local wildlife, camping and cabin facilities, plus lodge hours and green fees.

SALTPETER CAVES

http://www.saltpeter-caves.com/

The deepest caves in the Hocking Hills region, this site includes nice pictures of the guided tours, links to local horseback riding and vacation cabins.

SCIOTO TRAIL

http://www.dnr.ohio.gov/odnr/parks/directory/SCIOTOTR.htm

This area of undisturbed woods serves as a refuge for wildlife and nature lovers just south of Chillicothe. Visit this web site to learn about boating on the nearby Scioto river, plus hiking trails within the park.

SECREST ARBORETUM-WOOSTER

Gopher://sun1.oardc.ohio-state.edu:70/00/aboutag/secrest

Maintained by the Ohio Agricultural Research and Development Center of the Ohio State University, this site gives a good description of the arboretum, seasonal highlights, and current research.

SHAWNEE STATE PARK

http://www.dnr.ohio.gov/odnr/parks/directory/SHAWNEE.htm

Stroll through the woods that once served as hunting grounds for the mighty Shawnee nation. This beautiful land nicknamed "Little Smokies" lies within Shawnee State Forest. Visit this web site for history of the native peoples that once called this land home. Read about the geology of these rolling hills, and find out what outdoor events are planned for the coming months.

SOUTH BASS ISLAND

http://www.dnr.ohio.gov/odnr/parks/directory/LAKEERIE.htm

A real summertime hotspot, South Bass Island hosts a web site with information about the natural area, history of the island, plus how to get there and area attractions.

STAN HYWET HALL AND GARDENS-AKRON

http://www.stanhywet.org/

Rose, fragrance and Japanese gardens plus a restored Tudor mansion are featured at this site. Check seasonal displays and classes offered to the public, special events, membership information, and the online museum store.

STONELICK STATE PARK

http://www.dnr.ohio.gov/odnr/parks/directory/STONELCK.htm

This small natural area in southwest Ohio offers camping, boating and quiet nature walks. Visit its web site for details on restrictions, events, and park office contacts.

STROUDS RUN STATE PARK

http://www.dnr.ohio.gov/odnr/parks/directory/STROUDS.htm

Located near Athens, this park hosts a web site describing the natural area, boating on Dow Lake, and bridle trails within the park.

SYCAMORE STATE PARK

http://www.dnr.ohio.gov/odnr/parks/directory/SYCAMORE.htm

Western Ohio is the home of this lovely park where visitors can fish and ride on horseback. Visit this site for details on recreational opportunities plus phone numbers and addresses for park offices.

TAR HOLLOW STATE PARK

http://www.dnr.ohio.gov/odnr/parks/directory/TARHOLLW.htm

Source of tar pine for early Ohio settlers, this park includes Pine Lake, offering fishing and boating to seasonal visitors. Visit this web site for history behind the natural area and its name, plus details on outdoor activities available in this lovely park.

TINKER'S CREEK STATE PARK

http://www.dnr.ohio.gov/odnr/parks/directory/TINKERS.htm

This natural area near Ravenna includes swamps and marshland. Check the park's web page for information about the wetlands, hiking trails and picnic facilities available.

VAN BUREN STATE PARK

http://www.dnr.ohio.gov/odnr.parks/directory/VANBUREN.htm

Located in northwestern Ohio, this small park includes Van Buren Lake and the fishing and boating opportunities it offers. Check the web site for background information on the park's history, a description of the natural area, its wildlife, and facilities.

WAHKEENA NATURE PRESERVE

http://www.ohiohistory.org/places/wahkeena/

Located on the edge of Hocking Hills, this large outdoor education area includes sandstone cliffs and hiking trails. Visit the preserve online to get a good description of the preserve, plus location information.

WAYNE NATIONAL FOREST

http://www.fs.fed.us/recreation/forest_descr/oh_r9_Wayne.html

This site explains the ecosystem, geography, and natural features of Ohio's sole national forest. Recreational opportunities both within the park and nearby are explained, as are nearby points of interest.

WEST BRANCH STATE PARK

http://www.dnr.ohio.gov/odnr/parks/directory/WESTBRNC.htm

Boaters and fishermen alike will love this park near Ravenna which includes a large lake with many forks. Visit the web site for complete information on park regulations and facilities.

WOLF RUN STATE PARK

http://www.dnr.ohio.gov/odnr/parks/directory/wolfrun.htm

Located in southeastern Ohio, this park boasts Wolf Run Lake and all the water activities it affords. Check the web site for horsepower restrictions, which fish make the best catch, and natural history of the surrounding area.

WOOD COUNTY PARK DISTRICT

http://wcnet.org/~wcpd

History of the park system, upcoming programs and special events, plus a list of reservable shelters are highlighted.

XX. KIDS

OH!Kids! Wait till you see what Ohio has in store for you. These Ohio-grown web pages will take you to homework help, kids clubs, cartoons, coloring books, and games, then link you to your favorite sites around the country.

COOL THINGS FOR KIDS

http://www.ramlink.net/kidstuff.html
This is a great page posted by Ramnet, an Ohio Internet provider, and available to anyone via the web. Links to all the favorite kids sites including Crayola, Yahooligans, the Discovery Channel, Dr. Seuss, Goosebumps, and Disney.

DR. GOOP'S HOME PAGE

http://www.childrenshospital.columbus.oh.us/goop1.html
Designed for children and young adults with insulin-dependent diabetes, this site is maintained by the Childrens Hospital of Columbus and is intended to help children stick to their doctor's treatment plan. Interactive workshops with Dr. Goop help kids manage their disease, and enable them to hear what others their age are feeling and thinking.

DRAGONFLY

http://miavx1.muohio.edu/~dragonfly/

These interactive science lessons and activities for kids from Miami University correlate to Dragonfly Magazine, *which is published by the National Science Teachers' Association.*

EOS for Kids

http://www.eos.net/eos4kids/index.html

Cool sites close to Cincinnati and across the country, educational sites, plus Britannica Online. Includes links to COSI, the Cincinnati Zoo, Cedar Point, Sea World, NASA, Bill Nye the Science Guy, and the Discovery Channel.

Greater Cincinnati Kidstuff

http://www.insiders.com/cincinnati/main-kidstuff.htm

Posted by the editors of the Insiders Guide *travel series, this site follows the chapter format including outdoor playground listings, holiday tips, major attractions, and youth sports.*

Internet Ohio Links for Kids

http://www.ohio.net/kidslink.htm

Online reference books, games, coloring books, and cartoons.

Just 4 Kids

http://www.ohio-usa.com/ajeh/justkids.html

Stories, educational sites, animals, and the ever popular Beanie Babies.

MANSFIELD ONLINE KIDS LINK

http://www.mfdonline.com/kidslink.htm

Not just for kids, this list of links includes the Road Runner home page, web sites for teachers, Disneyland, and the High School News Web.

MEDINA COUNTY DISTRICT LIBRARY FOR KIDS

http://www.medina.lib.oh.us/kidshome.htm

Links to the OPLIN kids page, and other staff-selected goodies, plus information on library programs for kids and tips for parents with cyberkids.

MENTOR PUBLIC LIBRARY KIDSLINKS

http://www.mentor.lib.oh.us/kdslinks.html

Lots of great links for both parents and kids, including Sesame Street, the Smithsonian, the San Diego Zoo, and the Exploratorium in San Francisco.

MID-OHIO VALLEY KIDS PAGE

http://www.movnet.com/Kidsite.htm

Fun and educational sites for children, including sports sites, online activities, science, music, books, and coloring pages.

ODS KIDS!

http://www.ohio-distinctive.com/kids.html

This Ohio software company invites kids to try their products out online, including games, puzzles, and other fun activities to download.

OHIO HISTORICAL SOCIETY TIME TRAVELERS

http://winslo.ohio.gov/ohswww/traveler/kidindex.html

Travel back in time across Ohio history in this interactive site for kids.

OPLIN OH!KIDS!

http://www.oplin.lib.oh.us

If your kids are bored with their homework assignments, introduce them to this site. With web pages geared for every age group from tots to teens, and homework help, exciting graphics and loads of both educational and recreational web sites to choose from, they just might get inspired to learn something. And when they're done, check out the resources section designed for parents, educators, and librarians.

WGTE ONLINE JUST FOR KIDS

http://www.wgte.org/Kids.html

This public television station in Toledo posts a kids page with links to cool shows, hot web sites, and a kids club.

WILLOUGHBY-EASTLAKE PUBLIC LIBRARY CHILDREN'S ROOM

http://www.wepl.lib.oh.us/kids.html

Cool links like Ocean Odyssey, Nintendo, and the Discovery Channel.

INDEX

Orange Frazer Press
www.orangefrazer.com